OECD ECONOMIC SURVEYS

1992-1993

ITALY

ORGANISATION FOR ECONOMIC CO-OPERATION AND DEVELOPMENT

ORGANISATION FOR ECONOMIC CO-OPERATION AND DEVELOPMENT

Pursuant to Article 1 of the Convention signed in Paris on 14th December 1960, and which came into force on 30th September 1961, the Organisation for Economic Co-operation and Development (OECD) shall promote policies designed:

- to achieve the highest sustainable economic growth and employment and a rising standard of living in Member countries, while maintaining financial stability, and thus to contribute to the development of the world economy;
- to contribute to sound economic expansion in Member as well as non-member countries in the process of economic development; and
- to contribute to the expansion of world trade on a multilateral, non-discriminatory basis in accordance with international obligations.

The original Member countries of the OECD are Austria, Belgium, Canada, Denmark, France, Germany, Greece, Iceland, Ireland, Italy, Luxembourg, the Netherlands, Norway, Portugal, Spain, Sweden, Switzerland, Turkey, the United Kingdom and the United States. The following countries became Members subsequently through accession at the dates indicated hereafter: Japan (28th April 1964), Finland (28th January 1969), Australia (7th June 1971) and New Zealand (29th May 1973). The Commission of the European Communities takes part in the work of the OECD (Article 13 of the OECD Convention).

3 2280 00497 9803

Publié également en français.

Table of contents

Introduction   9

I. Recent developments   11

The descent into recession   11
The widening of labour market slack   13
The deepening of structural labour market imbalances   16
The policy response   19
Reduced wage- and consumer-price inflation   20
Improving the external balance   24

II. Macroeconomic policies and prospects   32

Monetary policy   32
Fiscal policy   38
Prospects   47

III. The drive for privatisation and structural reform   53

The public enterprise sector   54
The privatisation process   66
The economic and financial consequences of the privatisation plan   79
Financial market reform   95

IV. Conclusions   100

Notes and references   106

Annexes

I. Italy's public enterprise sector: an historical review   116
II. Supporting statistical material to Part III   129
III. Chronology of main economic events   145

Statistical and structural annex   153

Tables

Text

1. Unemployment rate   16
2. Indicators of labour-market performance at the peak of the cycle   18
3. Current account of the balance of payments   25
4. Hourly labour costs in manufacturing in EC countries   29
5. Net capital movements   31
6. Budget deficit targets and estimated outcomes in 1992   39
7. State borrowing requirements in 1992 – summary of trend and target values   39
8. General Government income statement   40
9. Public sector budget deficits in 1992   41
10. Financing of State borrowing requirements, 1988-1992   43
11. State borrowing requirements in 1993 and 1994 – summary of trend and target values   45
12. Medium-term targets   48
13. Short-term projections   51
14. Acquisitions and sales of public enterprises, 1983-1992   59
15. Risk capital provided to conglomerates by the State, 1980-1992   71
16. Financial plans of IRI and ENI, 1993-1995   71
17. Timetable of privatisation process as of December 1993   76
18. IRI and ENI: Market environment of main non-financial subsidiaries, 1991   79
19. Costs and prices of public services   84
20. Comparative size and structure of financial markets, 1990   85
21. Comparative size of the stock market, 1991   86
22. Fresh capital raised by Italian companies in the Milan stock exchange, 1985-1992   87
23. Estimates of public assets and liabilities   90

Annexes

A1. Efficiency and quality of public services: selected indicators   130
A2. Labour productivity in public services   131
A3. Financial indicators for the main public enterprises, 1980-1992   132

A4. IRI and ENI: Financial indicators of main non-financial
    subsidiaries, 1991   133
A5. Financial indicators of main public banks, 1991   134
A6. Credits of public banks to public enterprises, 1989-1992   134
A7. IRI group privatisations, 1983-1992   135
A8. Weight of public enterprises in total employment of non-
    agricultural business sector by main branches of activity, 1988   135
A9. State holdings in industry and services in the major
    1 898 enterprises, 1991   136
A10. Presence of the State in finance and insurance, 1991   137
A11. State-owned enterprises in the business sector   138
A12. Structure and sectoral ramification of public conglomerates
    (non-financial)   140
A13. Public services   142
A14. Main public enterprises listed in Italian and foreign stock
    markets, 1993   144

Statistical and structural annex

Selected background statistics   154
A. Expenditure on gross domestic product, current prices   155
B. Expenditure on gross domestic product, constant 1985 prices 156
C. Gross domestic product by kind of activity   157
D. Household appropriation account   158
E. General Government account   159
F. Prices and wages   160
G. Employment indicators   161
H. Money and credit   162
I. Foreign trade by main commodity groups   164
J. Geographical breakdown of foreign trade   165
K. Balance of payments   166
L. Public sector   167
M. Financial markets   168
N. Labour market indicators   169
O. Production structure and performance indicators   170

5

Diagrams

Text

1. Contribution to GDP growth   12
2. Business indicators   14
3. Sectoral employment trends   15
4. Short-run real wage rigidity and unemployment increase   17
5. Wage and price trends   21
6. Sectoral wage developments   22
7. Foreign-trade and consumer prices   26
8. International indicators of competitiveness   27
9. Export competitiveness and export performance   28
10. Relative price levels in 1990 between Italy and the EC   30
11. Interest rates   34
12. Exchange rate and interest rate developments   36
13. The public debt/GDP ratio and its components   42
14. Weight of public enterprises in the non-agricultural business sector
    of EC countries   56
15. Employment share of public enterprises in Italy and the EC by
    main branches   57
16. The evolution of public enterprises in the non-agricultural business
    sector, 1981-1990   58
17. Control channels and ownership linkages: before and after
    1992-1993 reforms   60
18. Management of privatisations   73
19. Selected indicators of comparative performance of non-financial
    firms   81
20. Indicators of sectoral performance, 1991   83
21. Composition of financial savings by household, 1991   85
22. Planned privatisations in Europe   96

Annexes

A1. Employment changes in public and private enterprises, 1969-1991   119
A2. Electricity tariffs   122

6

BASIC STATISTICS OF ITALY

THE LAND

Area (1 000 sq. km)	301.3	Inhabitants in major cities, 1.1.90, thousands:	
Agricultural area (1 000 sq. km), 1982	236.3	Rome	2 804
		Milan	1 449
		Naples	1 204
		Turin	1 003

THE PEOPLE

Population, 1.1.92, thousands	57 193		Thousands
Number of inhabitants per sq. km	190	Labour force, 1992	24 612
Net natural increase average (1987-91, thousands)	26	Employment, 1992	21 271
Net rate per 1 000 inhabitants (1987-91)	0.5	In agriculture	1 749
		In industry	6 850
		In services	12 670

PRODUCTION

Gross domestic product, 1992		Origin of gross domestic product in 1992 at market prices, per cent of total:	
(trillion of lira)	1 507		
GDP per head (1992 US$)	21 387	Agriculture	4.1
Gross fixed capital formation		Industry	29.0
Per cent of GDP in 1992	19.1	Construction	5.9
Per head in 1992 (US$)	4 088	Other	61.0

THE PUBLIC SECTOR

Public consumption, in 1992		Public debt in 1992 (percentage of GDP)	108.0
(percentage of GDP)	17.7	General government investment in 1992	
Current revenue of general government in 1992		(percentage of total investment)	19.2
(percentage of GDP)	47.3		

FOREIGN TRADE

Exports of goods and services as percentage of GDP, 1992	18.1	Imports of goods and services as a percentage of GDP, 1992	18.3
Major export categories, as a percentage of total exports, 1992 (SITC)	.	Main imports categories, as a percentage of total imports, 1992 (SITC)	
Machinery (71 to 77)	29.2	Food stuffs (0)	8.1
Fabric and textile goods (65)	5.3	Machinery (71 to 77)	20.9
Chemical products (5)	7.9	Metals, ores and scrap (67 +68)	8.5
Automobiles and parts (78 + 79)	4.4	Mineral fuels (3)	10.7
Mineral fuels (3)	2.1	Chemical products (5)	12.5

THE CURRENCY

Monetary unit: Lira		Currency units per US$, average of daily figures:	
		Year 1992	1 232
		September 1993	1 569

Note: An international comparison of certain basic statistics is given in an Annex table.

This Survey is based on the Secretariat's study prepared for the annual review of Italy by the Economic and Development Review Committee on 6th October 1993.

•

After revisions in the light of discussions during the review, final approval of the Survey for publication was given by the Committee on 28th October 1993.

•

The previous Survey of Italy was issued in December 1992.

Introduction

The speed and depth of political change which Italy has undergone since mid-1992 have defied all predictions. In a series of rapid steps, the country has unearthed a system of political corruption which for many years had squandered huge amounts of resources. The electorate in a referendum strongly favoured a switch to a majority-based voting system, which Parliament adopted in August. The referendum came out in favour of a reduction in the State's role in economic activities, supporting attempts by the Government to create a framework for large-scale privatisation. This political mandate was given to the Government at a time of recession, notwithstanding a surge in net exports spurred by currency depreciation since September 1992.

The fall in output, which began in the autumn of 1992, seems to have bottomed out in the summer, largely as a result of the rebound of exports. Internally, a collapse of consumer and business confidence this year depressed the level of domestic demand: private consumption declined in the face of real wage losses, while gloomier output prospects accelerated the decline in gross fixed investment. Overall, opposing developments between external and internal demand may leave the level of real GDP broadly unchanged in 1993, after a modest gain of about 1 per cent in 1992. The recovery of economic activity projected for 1994 and into 1995 would be too modest to reverse the rising trend of unemployment. Measures of income restraint combined with tight monetary conditions should contain the price-raising effects of the lira's fall, holding the rise in consumer prices to some 4 per cent in 1994.

Keeping inflation on a downward path and rolling back the huge budget deficit are key objectives of the new Government which took office in April 1993. Progress in these areas will crucially depend upon swift institutional reforms needed to rebuild confidence. The change to a new electoral (majority-based) system in August is a first important step in this direction. The new medium-term economic programme presented in July 1993 continues the policy of fiscal stringency. The additional measures of fiscal restraint should bring the 1993 budget deficit in line with the initial target, following several years of major fiscal slippage. In a climate of greater political stability, the floating exchange rate has bounced back from a historical low in early April 1993, settling around a level which implies a fall in the nominal effective exchange rate of over 20 per cent since September 1992. In this setting, interest rates eased further, led by repeated cuts in official lending rates.

The present Survey begins with a review of recent developments and discusses the post-election outlook in the light of the 1994 budget proposals and new measures of structural reform (Part I). Monetary trends are discussed against the background of the flexible exchange rate, which assigns to monetary aggregates a greater role in the formation of inflation expectations. Output and inflation prospects are evaluated against the background of the 1994 budget and the new medium-term stabilisation plan (Part II). The special chapter of this Survey (Part III) is devoted to privatisation, which should enhance overall economic efficiency and help meet the Maastricht convergence rules. Part IV summarises the key points of the Survey and offers some policy considerations.

I. Recent developments

Since the second half of 1989, Italy like many other countries has experienced a marked slowdown in economic growth. With high interest rates and, until September 1992, a rising real exchange rate, the level of demand has fallen increasingly short of output capacity. Confidence gains built up after the lira joined the narrow band of the European Monetary System (EMS) in January 1990 diminished with the failure of the Government to arrest the deteriorating trend of public finance. Risk premia in domestic interest rates widened as a consequence, complicating the already complex task of fiscal consolidation. Heavy losses in official reserves forced the Government to devalue the lira in September 1992 and to suspend its participation in the Exchange Rate Mechanism (ERM) of the EMS.

The descent into recession

In the closing months of 1992, the Italian economy dipped into recession, with GDP contracting by an annualised 1.2 per cent in the second half of 1992, the first decline since 1982. Pulled down by falling gross fixed investment and lower net exports, the rise in real GDP slipped below 1 per cent for the calendar year 1992, nearly half a percentage point below the EC average. Falling rates of return on capital, high real interest rates and a worsening business climate depressed fixed investment.[1] Private consumption levelled off in the second half of the year under the combined impact of falling real wages, growing labour market slack and deteriorating consumer confidence.[2] As a result, the level of domestic demand began to decline, pushing up unemployment from already high structural levels. The growth performance in 1992 would have been even weaker, had it not been for the unusual speed with which imports responded to the lira depreciation. As a result, the negative contribution of the real foreign balance to GDP growth decreased markedly in 1992 (Diagram 1).

Diagram 1. **CONTRIBUTION TO GDP GROWTH**
As a percentage of GDP in the previous year

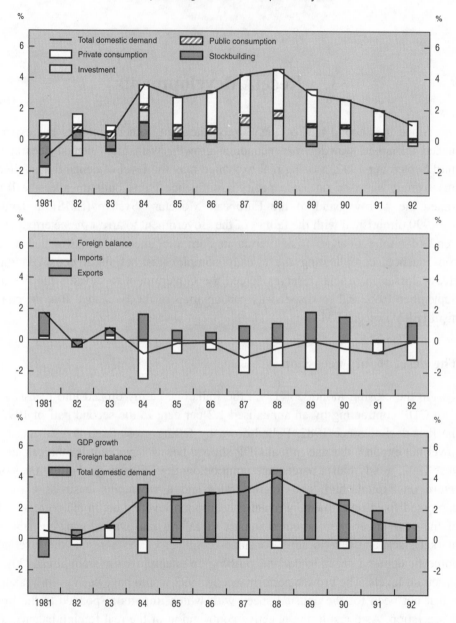

Source: OECD, *National Accounts.*

The economic downturn gathered pace in the autumn of 1992, as private consumption expenditure began to decline, compounding the drop in fixed investment, which had commenced earlier in the year. Several factors contributed to the fall in private consumption: increased taxation, pessimism about income growth and employment prospects and fears of capital losses on Government securities. By the end of 1992, industry had moved into deep recession: industrial value-added fell at a seasonally-adjusted annual rate of 2.1 per cent in the second half of 1992 and industrial investment for the year as a whole declined by more than 9 per cent. With stocks of finished goods reduced to more normal levels and foreign demand picking up in response to the currency depreciation, the contraction has slowed down since the beginning of 1993, leaving industrial output in the first seven months of the year 4.7 per cent lower than a year earlier. Capacity utilisation, at 75 per cent, was 2 percentage points lower (Diagram 2).

The widening of labour market slack

In an attempt to restore profitability, large industrial firms (employing 500 persons and more) reduced employment by nearly 6 per cent over the 12 months to mid-1993, notably blue-collar jobs. The number of hours compensated by the Wage Supplementation Fund (Cassa Integrazione Guadagni, CIG)[3] surged, rising by 23 per cent in the first eight months of 1993 over the same period of the previous year. Labour shedding also spread to the service sector, interrupting a long-standing upward employment trend, which has raised the service share, including public administration, to almost 60 per cent (Diagram 3). Within services, the retail and wholesale trade, notably self-employed, suffered most from employment losses. Banks, insurance companies and other financial institutions kept on hiring people, albeit at a reduced rate, stimulated by the progressive reform of financial markets (see below). With agricultural employment continuing its trend decline, overall employment shrank by 0.6 per cent in 1992, the worst employment outcome since 1972.

The labour force decreased in the course of 1992, partly in response to the worsening job prospects. Even so, according to previous definitions of employment and unemployment, the rate of unemployment jumped by nearly 2 percentage points to 13.1 per cent between the first and the fourth quarters of 1992 (Table 1). A new methodology used by ISTAT since October 1992 shows a much

13

Diagram 2. **BUSINESS INDICATORS**

Results of business surveys

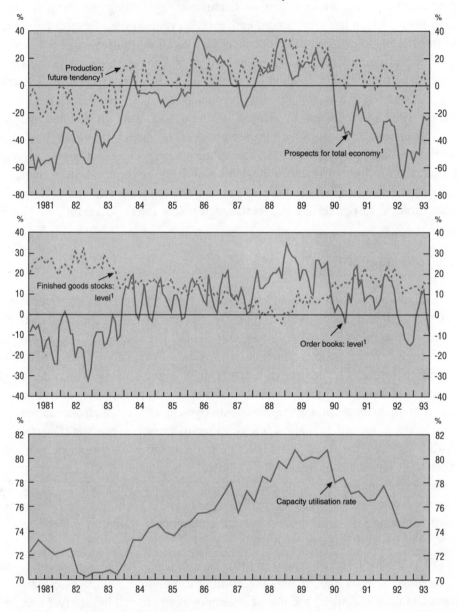

1. Per cent balance of positive and negative answers.
Source: OECD, *Main Economic Indicators.*

Diagram 3. **SECTORAL EMPLOYMENT TRENDS**

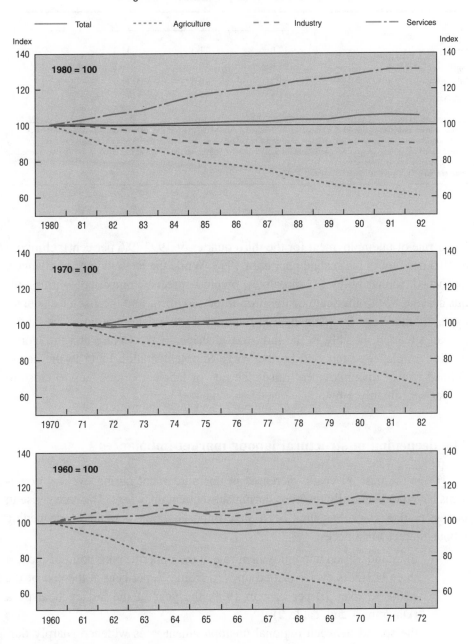

Table 1. **Unemployment rate**

	1990	1991	1992	1993
January	12.0	11.3	11.3	9.4[1]
April	11.0	10.9	10.8	10.5[1]
July	11.3	10.6	11.0	10.3[1]
October	11.3	11.0	13.1	
			9.6[1]	

1. Based upon new definitions of the labour force. Methodological changes include an extension of the list of branches of economic activity, a more detailed questionnaire and a re-definition of "job-seekers", counting as unemployed persons only those aged more than 15 who were available for work and took at least one initiative to find a job in the 30 days preceding the quarterly labour force survey.

Source: ISTAT, *Indicatori Mensili*, August 1993.

lower rate of unemployment for the third quarter of 1992 (9.6 per cent), climbing to 10.5 per cent in the second quarter of 1993. While the methodological changes, motivated, primarily, by EC directives, preclude precise comparison with previous surveys,[4] both the scale of the drop in employment and the rise in disbursements by the Wage Supplementation Fund testify to a deterioration of the labour market situation, notably in the industrial districts of the Centre and the North. Adding employees supported by the Wage Supplementation Fund to the newly defined rate of unemployment raises the rate of labour-market slack to close to 12 per cent in July 1993.

The deepening of structural labour market imbalances

Over the past 30 years, increases in unemployment during cyclical downturns have not been fully reversed during subsequent upswings. The recent rise in labour market slack has thus been superimposed upon a trend of deepening labour market imbalances:

- the standardised unemployment rate at the upper turning point of the last three business cycles drifted upward from 5½ per cent at the end of the 1960s to over 10 per cent in 1990, the year of the last cyclical peak (Diagram 4 and Table 2);
- the spread between regional unemployment rates widened sharply during the 1980s, with the rate in the South exceeding that in the North by

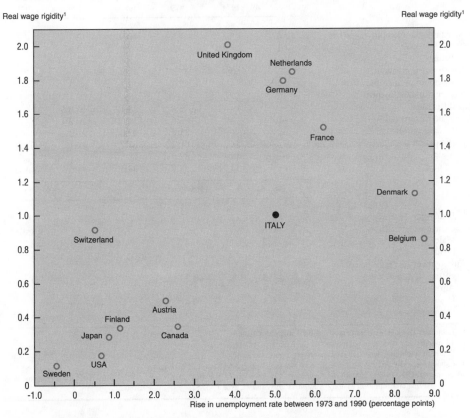

Diagram 4. **SHORT-RUN REAL WAGE RIGIDITY AND UNEMPLOYMENT INCREASE**

Real wage rigidity[1]

Real wage rigidity[1]

United Kingdom

Netherlands

Germany

France

Denmark

ITALY

Switzerland

Belgium

Austria

Finland

Japan

Canada

USA

Sweden

Rise in unemployment rate between 1973 and 1990 (percentage points)

1. Short-run real wage rigidity is measured by the amount of additional unemployment (as per cent of the labour force) needed to offset the short-term wage impact of a one percentage point price shock.
Source: OECD, 1989.

as much as 14½ percentage points in 1990. The differential has been even larger for female unemployment rates;

- while the share of unemployed persons of less than 25 years in total unemployment declined in the 1980s, that of long-duration unemployment (twelve months and over) surged, exceeding 50 per cent in 1990;

- structural labour market imbalances have worsened more for women than for men. At 17 per cent in 1990, the female unemployment rate was

17

Table 2. **Indicators of labour-market performance at the peak of the cycle**

	1968	1974	1979	1989	1990	1991
Standardised unemployment rate	5.6	5.3	7.6	10.9	10.3	9.9
Male	4.1	3.5	4.8	7.9	7.3	–
Female	9.3	9.4	13.2	18.6	17.1	–
Youth unemployment [1]	–	60.8	49.5	48.4	–	
Long-duration unemployment [2]	–	–	32.5	52.1	51.2	–
Regional unemployment differential [3]	–	–	6.4	15.1	14.6	–
Male differential [3]	–	–	3.6	11.6	10.7	–
Female differential [3]	–	–	11.1	23.0	23.2	–
Participation rates [4]	–	58.7	60.2	61.2	61.1	61.3
Male	–	85.1	82.6	78.5	78.1	78.3
Female	–	33.7	38.7	44.3	44.5	44.7

	1960-68	1968-73	1973-79	1979-90
Labour force (average percentage change at annual rate)	–0.6	–0.2	1.1	0.8
Male	–0.2	–0.4	0.3	0.2
Female	–1.5	0.5	2.9	1.8
Employment (average percentage change at annual rate)	–0.3	–0.3	0.8	0.5
Agriculture	–4.9	–4.7	–2.5	–4.1
Industry	0.8	0.4	0.3	–0.9
Services	1.4	1.3	2.7	2.5

1. Less than 25 years as a percentage of total unemployment.
2. 12 months and over as a percentage of total unemployment.
3. Southern unemployment rate minus northern unemployment rate.
4. Labour force divided by the population of working age (15-64 years) at mid-year.
Sources: OECD (1992), *Employment Outlook*; Commission of the European Communities (1993), "The Economic and Financial Situation in Italy", *Reports and Studies*, No. 1, p. 52.

nearly 10 percentage points higher than the male rate. This compares with a differential of 5 percentage points at the end of the 1960s.

The incidence of structural unemployment, concentrated among young people and women living in the South, reflects a number of institutional factors: sector-specific, centralised wage bargaining, restrictive employment rules, and rather generous transfer payments to large segments of companies and households, keeping the supply price of labour relatively high. As analysed in earlier OECD Surveys,[5] each of these three factors has reduced regional labour mobility. Lay-off and recruitment restrictions were until recently judged to be the most stringent ones in the EC.[6] By making sectoral wage accords applicable to all regions, notwithstanding large differences in levels of labour productivity, centralised wage bargaining has contributed to the rigidity of wage differentials. And generous tax expenditure and transfer payments to a large number of firms and households together with the large "black economy" have negatively affected market-clearing mechanisms and adjustments. Taken together, all these characteristics have made Italy's labour market one of the least flexible in the EC.[7]

The policy response

A number of important measures have, however, been taken in recent years to enhance the flexibility of the labour market, most prominent among them the abolition of the job allocation scheme in July 1991,[8] the suspension and subsequent removal of the wage indexation scheme, *scala mobile* in December 1991 and July 1992, and the new labour agreement in July 1993. Seeking greater support of employers and trade unions for policy targets, the agreement of July 1993 explicitly mentions a reduction of inflation, cuts in the budget deficit and exchange rate stability as primary goals of incomes policy. Signed by the Government, trade unions and the employers' organisation and endorsed by the work force, the new labour accord lays out a new framework for industrial relations and wage bargaining. It has effectively replaced Italy's three-pronged system of wage determination in the private sector, under which wage increases consisted of an indexation payment (national component), an industry-wide component and firm-specific payments. Applicable to private employees, the accord is likely to moderate wage claims in upcoming wage negotiations, both in the private and public sector. Its main points are:

- a four-year national labour contract regulates labour relations, while nominal wages will be renegotiated every two years, keeping the overall rise within the **projected** rate of consumer-price inflation (national component of wage increases);
- over and above inflation-determined pay increases, individual companies may raise wages only to reflect higher profits and productivity gains (company component of wage increases);

- Government, employers and trade unions will meet twice a year (May-June and September) to agree on objectives for inflation, growth and employment;
- during periods in which new national wage contracts are being negotiated, wage increases will remain below projected inflation;
- the hiring of trainees and apprentices will be simplified and entry wages lowered. Companies will be able to hire employees on a temporary basis from new employment agencies to be established or to "rent out" labour;
- access to payments from the Wage Supplementation Fund will be widened to include services, and lay-off payments extended to small companies and disbursement of benefits to temporarily laid-off people speeded up.[9]

In addition, other measures affecting the labour market have begun to be put into effect. They include the reform of both the public labour market and social benefit provisions (pensions and health benefits; see Part II) as well as action to roll back the influence of organised crime and a new stance on regional policy. Recent legislation has terminated special intervention in favour of the South. Support to disadvantaged areas will now be given on the basis of common nation-wide criteria in conformity with EC rules.[10] Faced with rising unemployment, the Government in August 1993 took action to accelerate L 10 trillion of spending on public works, especially transport infrastructure and new buildings.

Reduced wage- and consumer-price inflation

Nominal wage growth continued to subside in 1993, with the 12-month increase in the hourly wage rate falling to 2.6 per cent in August 1993, about 4 percentage points below the rate recorded a year earlier and 1.8 points below the rate of consumer-price inflation (Diagram 5). Until spring 1993, the pace of wage disinflation was more pronounced in industry and the public administration than in some service sub-sectors, where nominal wage growth still exceeded the rise in consumer prices (Diagram 6). Apart from the weakening of labour markets, the moderation of nominal wages owed much to the Incomes Policy Accord

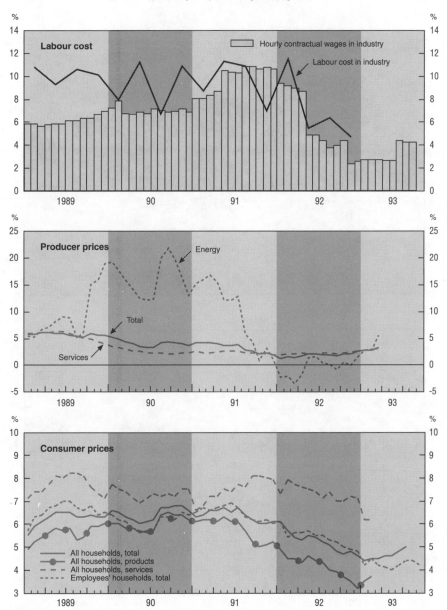

Diagram 5. **WAGE AND PRICE TRENDS**

Year-on-year percentage changes

Sources: ISTAT, ISCO.

21

Diagram 6. **SECTORAL WAGE DEVELOPMENTS[1] AND CONSUMER PRICES**

Year-on-year growth rate, 3-month moving average

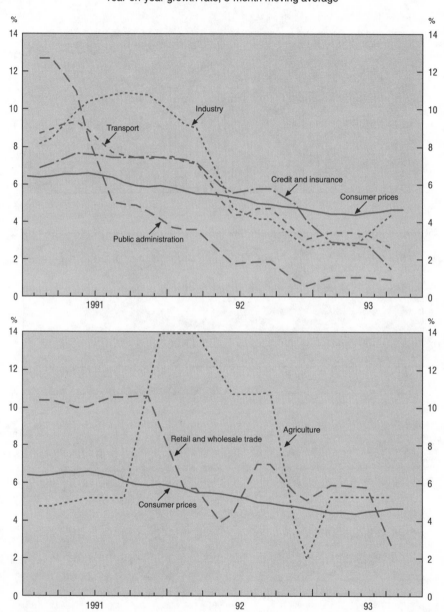

1. Contractual hourly earnings.
Source: ISTAT, *Monthly Indicators,* various issues.

of July 1992. In addition, the Government suspended the renewal of public-sector contracts until January 1994 (Diagram 6). More recently, nominal wage growth in industry began to rise, reflecting staged pay increases agreed upon under old wage contracts.

The deceleration of nominal wage growth in 1992 and in the first half of 1993 went hand-in-hand with large-scale labour shedding, notably in industry. As a result, the rise in **unit labour costs** was more than halved, falling from 7.6 per cent in 1991 to 4.2 per cent in 1992 and to 3 per cent in the first half of 1993. Contained by the ERM and the weakening state of demand, both externally and domestically, the year-on-year rise in **industrial producer prices** fell to a record low of 1.9 per cent in the third quarter of 1992. The lira depreciation reversed the falling trend, however, pushing the 12-month rate up to 4.1 per cent in June 1993. The re-acceleration of inflation was more marked at the level of **wholesale prices**, reflecting a surge in prices for imported intermediate products.

In contrast to producer and wholesale prices, **consumer prices** kept on decelerating through the first nine months of 1993, reflecting wage moderation, flagging demand, the freeze of public utility charges from summer 1992, and, more generally, a downward shift in inflationary expectations. Moreover, to preserve market shares in Italy, foreign suppliers accepted cuts in their profit margins immediately after the lira depreciation and the rise in import prices that took place in lira terms was not fully passed on to consumers. In October, the 12-month rate of consumer-price inflation stood at 4.2 per cent, about 1 point below the pre-devaluation level.

Relatively high price increases for **private services**, in part a consequence of barriers to competition,[11] limited inflation convergence with core EMS-countries. Widening since early 1991, the differential between price rises for consumer services and consumer goods exceeded 3 percentage points in late 1992, but narrowed sharply thereafter, partly reflecting efficiency gains in the distribution sector. To bring **VAT rates** in line with EC rules, the Government modified the system of indirect taxes at the end of 1992, replacing the low excise tax for food products by the standard 19 per cent rate, taxing cigarettes, sugar and coffee more heavily, and abolishing the 38 per cent rate on luxury goods. The revision is expected to have little effect on the average level of prices.[12]

Improving the external balance

Over the past 18 months or so, balance-of-payments developments have been dominated by violent swings in speculative capital movements and marked changes in relative competitive positions. Over the nine months to September 1992, a collapse of investors' confidence, linked to fiscal slippage and political instability, produced huge outflows of non-bank capital. Even though domestic interest rates rose from already high levels, the induced influx of short-term capital proved insufficient to cover the widening deficits on current and long-term capital accounts. In the event, heavy losses in official reserves made an exchange rate adjustment unavoidable: a 7 per cent official devaluation of the lira against other currencies of the EMS in September 1992 was followed a few days later by a suspension of the lira's participation in the ERM, resulting in a further depreciation of the currency.

Subsequently, deprived of its ERM-anchor, the exchange rate fluctuated sharply, reflecting recurrent unrest on international currency markets as well as political uncertainties. In May 1993, its steepening decline was reversed by the formation of a new Government, following the April referendum about institutional reform. The exchange-rate weakened again in August following modifications of the ERM.[13] The currency depreciation quickly improved the trade balance, shifting the current account balance into surplus in the first half of 1993. With a return of non-bank capital, the capital account swung back into huge surplus, permitting the Bank of Italy to recoup part of its sizeable losses in international reserves.

Current account developments

In 1992, the **current account deficit** increased by nearly L 6 trillion to L 33 trillion or 2.3 per cent of GDP, the biggest deficit since 1981 (Table 3). The deterioration was in large measure attributable to continued losses in competitiveness, which pushed up the trade deficit (balance-of-payments basis) in the first half of the year and reduced the traditional surplus of tourism. The growth of import volumes, after quickening in the first half of 1992, levelled off in the second half of the year, curbed by the deepening recession and currency depreciation. Following the floating of the lira, foreign suppliers reduced profit margins, thereby damping the depreciation-induced rise in import prices. With exports

Table 3.   **Current account of the balance of payments**

Trillions of lire

	1987	1988	1989	1990[1]	1991	1992
Exports (f.o.b.)	150.3	165.8	192.2	202.6	208.9	218.8
Imports (f.o.b.)	150.7	167.3	195.1	202.0	209.8	215.7
Trade balance	−0.4	−1.5	−3.0	0.6	−0.9	3.1
Investment income, credits	8.3	9.7	14.5	19.4	25.2	30.5
Investment income, debits	16.9	18.9	25.9	35.3	45.2	56.2
Investment income, net	−8.6	−9.3	−11.4	−15.9	−20.0	−25.7
Foreign travel, credits	15.8	16.1	16.4	23.7	22.9	
Foreign travel, debits	5.9	7.8	9.3	16.6	14.5	
Foreign travel, net	9.9	8.3	7.2	7.1	8.4	6.7
Other services, credits	24.8	26.4	32.6	47.7	44.2	
Other services, debits	23.9	28.4	37.8	53.4	55.7	
Other services, net	0.9	−2.0	−5.2	−5.7	−11.6	−8.9
Private transfers, net	1.7	1.9	1.8	1.0	−1.5	−2.0
Official transfers, net	−2.9	−3.7	−4.8	−4.0	−5.8	−5.0
Current balance	−1.4	−7.5	−14.8	−17.6	−26.3	−32.8

1. Liberalisation of capital control has induced a break in 1990 for the series of foreign travel and other services.
Source: Bank of Italy (1993), *Assemblea Generale Ordinaria dei Partecipanti*, May.

rebounding in response to the lira depreciation, the trade balance swung into surplus in the second half of 1992. Thanks to an extraordinarily quick reaction of trade volumes, the trade balance closed with a small surplus for 1992 as a whole (Table 3). The trade surplus continued to widen in the first half of 1993, thanks to buoyant export volumes.

Prior to the floating of the lira, **import penetration** showed a marked rise in most areas of demand, leading to growing trade deficits in key sectors like transport equipment, chemical products and ferrous and non-ferrous ores and metals, and shrinking surpluses in textiles, leather products and clothing, metal products and machinery. **Sales in foreign markets** suffered from declining price competitiveness, weak demand and a lack of product differentiation.[14] As a result, the value of goods exports (balance-of-payments basis) remained virtually flat over the eighteen months to mid-1992. Thereafter, the sharply falling exchange rate created room for a substantial rise in lira export prices, which together with the quick reaction of export volumes to lower prices in foreign currency shifted the trade balance into surplus in the second half of 1992 (Diagram 7). Largely thanks to surging exports outside the EC, the trade balance strengthened further in the first half of 1993.

The average decline in the nominal effective exchange rate of 20 per cent since September 1992 far exceeded the cumulative loss in cost **competitiveness** incurred since 1987 (Diagram 8). Such losses had diminished with the accession to the narrow band of the ERM in January 1990 and the related imposition of a stronger exchange rate discipline. Indeed, over the 33 months to September 1992, when the lira was withdrawn from the ERM, relative unit labour costs in manufacturing, expressed in a common currency, had changed little. Nevertheless, the

Diagram 7. **FOREIGN-TRADE AND CONSUMER PRICES**

(s.a.a.r)

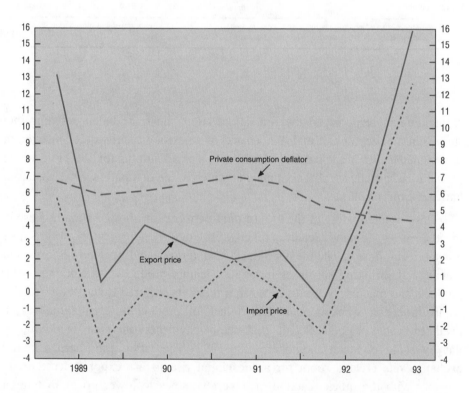

Source: OECD.

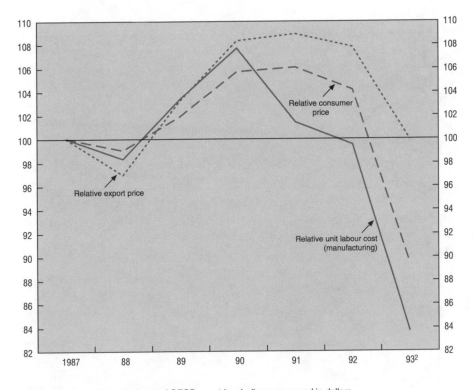

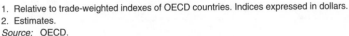

1. Relative to trade-weighted indexes of OECD countries. Indices expressed in dollars.
2. Estimates.
Source: OECD.

earlier deterioration in cost competitiveness and a continued rise in relative export prices (Diagram 8) led to a loss in market shares of 7¹/₂ percentage points between early 1990 and mid-1992 (Diagram 9), of which some part has already been recouped within the first year after the depreciation of the lira.

Comparing **levels of hourly labour costs in manufacturing** in EC countries suggests that prior to the EMS currency crisis in September 1992 the lira was overvalued. Total labour costs, including non-wage labour costs, which are exceptionally high, were next to Germany the highest among EC countries in

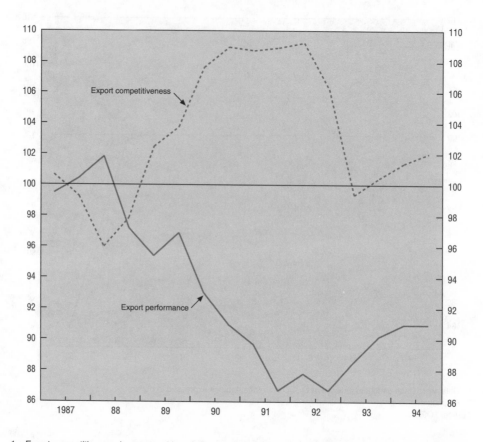

Diagram 9. **EXPORT COMPETITIVENESS AND EXPORT PERFORMANCE**[1]
1987 = 100

1. Export competitiveness is measured by relative export unit value of manufactured goods. Export performance is the ratio of Italy's export of manufactures to its export markets. From second half-year 1993 data are projections. *Source:* OECD.

1991 (Table 4). The recent currency depreciation together with wage restraint strongly improved Italy's position. Using **PPP for comparing levels of consumer prices** in 1990 reveals, on average, no substantial disadvantage *vis-à-vis* the EC, but points to relatively high prices for a number of services relevant to

Table 4. **Hourly labour costs in manufacturing
in EC countries**

Italy = 100

	1991	January 1993
Germany	125.3	140.2
Italy	**100.0**	**100.0**
Netherlands	99.4	117.2
Belgium	98.1	123.0
Denmark	96.2	112.6
France	82.2	114.9
United Kingdom	70.3	80.5
Spain	69.6	74.7
Ireland	67.1	89.7
Greece	34.2	36.8
Portugal	24.1	31.0

Sources: Bank for International Settlements (1992), *62nd Annual Report*, p. 126; CERC – Centre d'Études des Revenus et des Coûts (1993).

tourism (notably hotels and restaurants) (Diagram 10). PPP data for 1990 also suggest overvaluation for investment goods relative to the EC.

The decrease in competitiveness prior to the lira depreciation coincided with a steeply rising trend of **net interest payments on foreign debt**. The removal of the last vestiges of capital controls in May 1990 contributed to this development. In 1992, net outflows on investment income rose to 1.5 per cent of GDP, three times as large as the trade deficit, driven by further increases in the foreign debt and larger interest rate differentials *vis-à-vis* other major countries. Following the withdrawal of the lira from the ERM, the yield gap between Italy's external liabilities and external assets started to narrow, but in lira terms the deficit on net investment income has remained large.

Large swings of capital flows

Heightened uncertainties about political and economic developments led to large outflows of non-bank capital in 1992 (Table 5), which were more than offset by an influx of bank capital, attracted by high domestic interest rates. Foreign loans to Italy as well as foreign portfolio investment in Italy contracted, falling short of Italy's portfolio investment abroad. The picture changed substan-

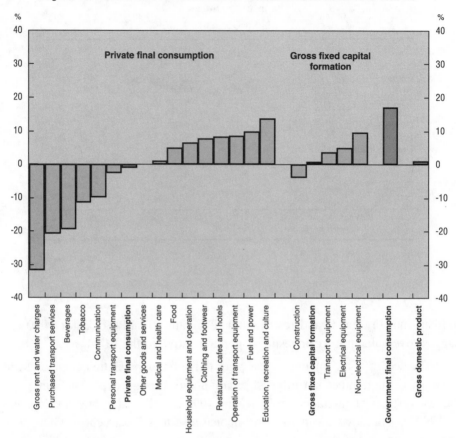

Diagram 10. **RELATIVE PRICE LEVELS IN 1990 BETWEEN ITALY AND THE EC[1]**

1. Defined as the percentage difference between the price level in Italy and the weighted average price level in EC countries.
Source: OECD, *Purchasing Power Parities and Real Expenditures,* 1992.

tially in the first seven months of 1993, with large amounts of non-bank capital returning, a sign of improved confidence.

The small deficit on capital account for 1992 concealed large swings during the year. Prior to the Danish referendum on the Maastricht Treaty at the beginning of June 1992, high domestic interest rates ensured inflows of bank capital far

Table 5. **Net capital movements**

Trillions of lire

	1987	1988	1989	1990	1991	1992
Total capital movements	11.2	21.7	34.2	52.1	28.8	11.8
Bank capital flows	5.6	10.2	15.0	23.0	39.4	25.3
Non-bank capital flows	5.6	11.4	19.2	29.2	-10.6	-13.5
Foreign direct investment in Italy	5.4	9.0	3.0	7.6	3.1	3.9
Italian direct investment abroad	-3.0	-7.2	-2.9	-9.1	-9.1	-7.3
Foreign portfolio investment in Italy	-4.8	7.5	17.1	23.0	23.2	12.8
Italian portfolio investment abroad	-4.8	-7.1	-12.4	-23.3	-30.8	-24.2
Foreign loans	12.3	11.2	19.9	36.2	13.4	9.1
Italian loans	-1.4	-2.3	-1.7	-4.8	-7.7	-5.9
Commercial credits and other items	2.0	0.4	-3.8	-0.4	-2.8	-1.9
Errors and omissions	-2.3	-3.2	-3.7	-19.1	-10.6	-11.6
Change in official reserves	-6.8	-10.9	-15.4	-15.2	8.6	32.5
Memorandum item: Level of official reserves in percentage of GDP	7.6	7.6	7.8	7.9	6.6	4.5

Source: Bank of Italy (1993), *Supplemento al Bollettino Statistico*, Bilancia dei Pagamenti.

in excess of non-bank capital outflows, a pattern already observed in 1991. Thereafter, expectations of currency depreciation produced a huge outflow of non-bank capital. With the lira floating, bank capital stopped flowing out of the country in the last quarter of 1992, while large amounts of exported non-bank capital returned to Italy. Official reserves in 1992 fell by almost a third, an amount close to the current account deficit, more than 2 per cent of GDP. The situation changed in the first half of 1993, when capital inflows more than offset the current account deficit. However, at L 67.6 trillion in mid-1993, the official foreign exchange reserves were still significantly below pre-depreciation levels.

II. Macroeconomic policies and prospects

In September 1992, only a few days after the lira was forced out of the ERM, the Amato Government announced a package of fiscal restraint for 1993 which has no parallel in Italy's recent budget history. Aware of the urgency of dealing with spiralling public debt, the Government requested and obtained from Parliament through a delegation law special powers to curb primary spending in four areas: public employment, pension benefits, health care and local authorities' finance. The firm determination of the Government to deal with the poor state of the public finances was also manifest in its readiness to take up a conditional loan from the EC in January 1993, subjecting budget plans to periodic reviews. The tighter fiscal stance facilitated the task of monetary policy to bring inflation into line with the best performing EC countries. Indeed, consumer-price inflation, displaying only mild effects from currency depreciation, continued to ease in 1993. The widening corruption scandal temporarily destabilised market sentiment. A new Government came into power in April 1993, following referendum results which called for large-scale institutional reform. Stepping up the efforts at structural reform, the new Government, headed by Mr. Ciampi, the former Governor of the Bank of Italy, has drawn up a realistic programme of fiscal stabilisation. This, together with the adoption of a new (majority-based) electoral law, has greatly improved the framework within which stabilisation policies operate.

Monetary policy

Since the autumn of 1992, monetary policy has been conducted in a new setting, marked by the lira's departure from the ERM, wide swings of the exchange rate and determined moves of two successive Governments to overcome the political crisis at home. Avoiding an exchange-rate-induced flare-up of inflation became the primary concern of the central bank. Greater attention was paid to controlling money supply and credit. The target range for M2 growth for 1993 was left unchanged at 5 to 7 per cent, notwithstanding prospective faster price rises triggered by the currency depreciation. In addition, in October 1992 the Bank of Italy called on the credit institutions to keep the rise in lira lending within confines set out in a six-month monitoring programme. At the same time, the central bank pursued its intermediate aim of steering high interest rates gradually down to levels more commensurate with the steady decline in inflation and the weak state of the economy. In the first half of 1993, the unexpectedly favourable inflation performance along with stabilisation initiatives taken by the new Government bolstered market confidence, setting the stage for further cuts in official lending rates. Legislation ending the Treasury's overdraft facility with the central bank was passed in November 1993.

Interest and exchange rate developments

Monetary conditions have eased substantially since the lira left the ERM. The Bank of Italy lowered the **discount rate** in nine steps from 15 per cent in September 1992 to 8 per cent in October 1993, the lowest rate since 1976, and the rate on fixed term advances (**Lombard rate** or *anticipazioni a scadenza fissa*) from 16.5 per cent to 9 per cent over the same period (Diagram 11). At this level, official rates were significantly lower than in December 1991, when expectations about the conduct of fiscal policy in 1992, an election year, began to worsen. Policy moves to steer interest rates down were suspended in March 1993, when fears of renewed fiscal slippage and political instability sent the exchange rate tumbling to new record lows. In April, the referendum results and a further easing of monetary policy in Germany paved the way for further cuts in official interest rates. In September, the target range for M2 growth was reaffirmed for 1994.

The step-wise reduction in key official lending rates was accompanied by a number of other measures, including the introduction in October 1992 of foreign currency swaps, which has widened the range of instruments available to the Bank of Italy to manage liquidity;[15] and, most importantly, a change in February 1993 in the system of **minimum reserve requirements**. The Bank of Italy lowered reserve requirements on most deposits from 22.5 per cent to 17.5 per cent with effect from 15 February, the start of the new reserve maintenance

Diagram 11. **INTEREST RATES**

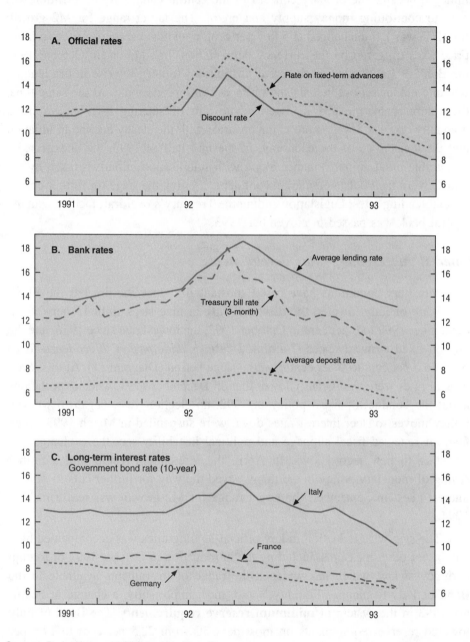

A. Official rates

Rate on fixed-term advances

Discount rate

1991   92   93

B. Bank rates

Average lending rate

Treasury bill rate
(3-month)

Average deposit rate

1991   92   93

C. Long-term interest rates
Government bond rate (10-year)

Italy

France

Germany

1991   92   93

Sources: Bank of Italy and OECD, Analytical Data Base.

period, and reduced to 10 per cent in March 1993 the reserve ratio on certificates of deposits (CDs) with maturities of eighteen months or more.[16] In addition, the fraction of compulsory reserves tradeable in the one-month maintenance period was raised from 5 per cent to 7 per cent. In July, interest paid on compulsory reserves against CDs was lowered to 6.5 per cent from 8.5 per cent. Overall, the reduction in minimum reserve requirements freed about L 34 trillion from compulsory reserves, allowing lending rates to ease by an estimated 35 to 40 basis points. Despite the reform, Italy's compulsory reserves remain well above those imposed by many other countries, putting Italian banks at a competitive disadvantage *vis-à-vis* banks abroad.[17]

Along with the deepening recession, disinflation and large cuts in official rates, the rate on short-term **interbank** deposits eased. Over the twelve months to October 1993, it dropped by about 10 percentage points, down to the levels of mid-1990, when remaining capital controls were abolished. In the process, the short-term interest rate differential *vis-à-vis* Germany narrowed to 2 percentage points in October 1993, compared with a differential of 7.4 points recorded a year earlier. While the interbank rate had already returned to mid-1992 levels by early 1993, minimum and average **bank lending rates** declined less rapidly, displaying downward stickiness in the face of greater insolvency risks in the corporate sector.

Long-term interest rates (on ten-year Government bonds), showing a more moderate reaction to the exchange-rate crisis than short-term rates, followed a gently declining trend from September 1992. While the slope of the **yield curve** for Government securities flattened from September 1992, the average net yield on Treasury bonds with a residual maturity of more than nine years was still higher in January 1993 than it had been in mid-1992, no doubt reflecting a depreciation-induced rise in inflation expectations. Even though long-term interest rates eased following the formation of the new Government in April,[18] in September 1993 they still exceeded comparable rates in Germany and France by 2 percentage points in nominal terms (Diagram 12).

The persistence of large risk premia in domestic interest rates reflected fears of rising inflation and additional currency depreciation. They may also have been kept high by heightened political uncertainties as **yields on Italy's foreign currency** issues exceeded those on issues of other sovereign borrowers and international organisations in the same currencies by 50 to 60 basis points.[19]

Diagram 12. **EXCHANGE RATE AND INTEREST RATE DEVELOPMENTS**

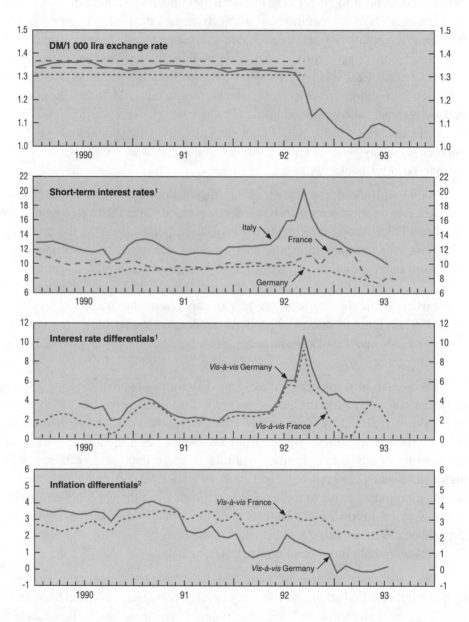

1. Inter-bank rate.
2. Inflation measured as consumer prices index.
Source: OECD, Analytical Data Base.

Since the formation of the new Government, a strengthening of market sentiment was reflected in a decline in the interest spread on foreign issues to 40 basis points in September.

M2 growth, after rising beyond the upper limit of the 5 to 7 per cent target range in the first half of 1992, abated during the following six months. Monetary expansion was reined in by a steep rise in interest rates during the three months to October and the deterioration of cyclical conditions. In September 1992, with capital outflows swelling and interest rates peaking, M2 growth moved towards the lower limit of the target range. The 12-month rate of M2 growth was 5.9 per cent in December 1992, the mid-point of the target range, rising to 6.8 per cent in August 1993. As had been the case in the previous two years, net direct financing of the Treasury by the central bank in 1992 was negative. While the Treasury drew nearly L 8 trillion on its overdraft facility with the central bank, the largest amount since 1988, the Bank of Italy in turn did not replace maturing Government securities held in its portfolio (about L 10 trillion). The annual growth of **domestic credit** to the non-state sector slowed sharply from 14 per cent in December 1991 to 7 per cent a year later, easing further to 1.4 per cent in September 1993. In contrast, domestic credit to the state sector kept on expanding strongly, as the State budget deficit even outstripped revised (looser) targets (see below).

The exchange rate showed wide gyrations after the withdrawal of the lira from the ERM in September 1992. In response to ambitious budget proposals for 1993 and continued disinflation, the **exchange rate** bounced back from a low of L 990 per Deutschemark in early October 1992, settling down within the L 850 to 900 range in November and December after official interest rates had been lowered. In January 1993, the authorities reconfirmed Italy's commitment to full monetary integration in the EC with the issue of DM 5 billion five-year bonds of the Republic of Italy and a loan from the European Community of ECU 8 billion, conditional on periodic EC reviews of the budgetary programme.[20] However, the return of relative calm in foreign-exchange markets proved transient: over the three months to April, growing apprehensions about Italy's political and economic future pushed the lira down to new historic lows against all major currencies, implying considerable undervaluation relative to standard measures of competitiveness (see Part I). From late April 1993, the lira recovered in response to the referendum results and the subsequent formation of a new Government. But in August it began losing ground again, following the widening of the ERM fluctuation bands.

Fiscal policy

Budget policy and outturn for 1992

A massive deficit overrun recurred in 1992, preventing a fall in **State Government borrowing requirement** relative to GDP. At L 163.1 trillion, the 1992 State budget deficit overshot the initial target by as much as L 35 trillion or 2.3 per cent of GDP, the biggest deviation among G7 countries (Tables 6 and 7). The budget outcome even exceeded the revised deficit target of L 150 trillion, notwithstanding new measures of fiscal restraint taken by the incoming Government in July 1992. As a result, State Government borrowing requirement (cash basis, including proceeds from privatisation) remained unchanged at 10.7 per cent of GDP. Yet, for the first time in nearly 30 years, the State primary (non-interest) balance swung into surplus, showing a small positive balance of 0.7 per cent of GDP as against a planned surplus of L 27 trillion or 1.8 per cent of GDP. Amounting to 1.5 per cent of GDP, the change in the cyclically adjusted primary balance implied a significant move towards fiscal restraint. On a general-Government basis, the primary surplus was equal to 1.4 per cent of GDP, the second best result among major countries.

The huge deficit overshoot in 1992 stemmed largely from lower-than-expected output growth, higher-than-expected interest rates and virtually no proceeds from privatisation. The deficit overrun would have been even bigger had it not been for unexpectedly high yields from one-off taxes on real estate and bank deposits and from fiscal amnesty (*condono tributario*). Underlying the initial 1992 budget proposals were projections of real GDP growth of 2.5 per cent, subsequently lowered to 1.8 per cent in March 1992, and an easing of consumer-price inflation to 4.5 per cent. As it turned out, output growth dropped to 1 per cent, whereas consumer-price inflation amounted to 5.4 per cent.

General Government borrowing requirements, excluding receipts from privatisation, eased to 10.2 per cent of GDP in 1992 from 10.8 per cent in 1991 (Table 8).[21] Thanks to additional measures of fiscal restraint taken in July and September 1992,[22] tax receipts advanced more rapidly than outlays, raising the

Table 6. **Budget deficit targets and estimated outcomes in 1992**

Per cent of GDP

	Level of government	Deficit overshoot	Primary deficit[1]
Italy	State	2.3	−1.4
France	Central	1.9	1.0
United Kingdom	Public sector	1.4	4.8
Canada	Federal	1.4	1.0
Japan	Central	0.5	−2.0
United States	Federal	0.3	2.5
Germany	Federal	−0.1	0.1

1. General government.
Source: OECD (1993), *Economic Outlook* No. 53, July, pp. 41 and 143.

Table 7. **State borrowing requirements in 1992 – summary of trend and target values**

	Trend		Target	
	Trillions of lire	Per cent of GDP	Trillions of lire	Per cent of GDP
Outcome 1991	152.3	10.7		
1992 Budget				
September 1991	183.0	12.2	127.8	8.5
Revenue increases			36.5	
Expenditure cuts and lower interest				
payments			25.0	
Total adjustment			61.5	
July 1992	180.0	12.0	150.0	10.0
Revenue increases			21.8	
Expenditure cuts			8.2	
Total adjustment			30.0	
Outcome 1992	163.1			
	159.0[1]	10.5		

1. Excluding financial needs of railways and other autonomous agencies, *Aziende autonome dello Stato*, the legal status of which was changed to that of a joint-stock company in 1992.
Sources: Ministero del Bilancio e della Programmazione Economica, *Relazione Previsionale e Programmatica,* September 1992; Bank of Italy (1993), *Economic Bulletin* No. 16, February.

Table 8.   **General Government income statement**

	Trillions of lire		Per cent changes	
	1991	1992	$\dfrac{1991}{1990}$	$\dfrac{1992}{1991}$
Expenditure				
Wages and salaries	205.8	216.3	8.9	5.1
Intermediate consumption	75.9	82.1	8.3	8.2
Social transfers	261.4	288.5	9.6	10.4
Production subsidies	22.7	23.8	17.6	4.8
Debt interest	147.4	173.4	15.7	17.6
Other	16.0	18.2	27.0	13.8
Total current expenditure	729.1	802.3	11.0	10.0
As a per cent of GDP	52.0	57.3		
Investment	52.5	55.3	4.4	5.3
Investment grants and other capital expenditure	11.8	10.3	..	−12.7
Total capital expenditure	64.3	65.6	−2.0	2.0
Total expenditure	793.4	868.0	9.8	9.4
As a per cent of GDP	56.7	57.1		
Revenue				
Direct taxes	209.1	248.6	10.0	18.9
Indirect taxes	160.0	169.4	14.5	5.9
Social security contributions	210.0	226.3	10.9	7.8
Other	60.7	64.8	16.5	6.8
Total current revenue	639.8	709.1	12.0	10.8
Capital revenue	2.3	3.1	7.0	34.8
Total revenue	642.1	712.3	11.9	10.9
As a per cent of GDP	45.7	47.5		
Net borrowing	151.3	155.7		
As a per cent of GDP	10.8	10.2		
Primary balance	−4.1	17.7		
As a per cent of GDP	0.3	1.2		

Source: Bank of Italy (1993), *Assemblea generale ordinaria dei partecipanti,* Appendice, May, pp. 122-123.

ratio of **general Government revenues** to GDP to an all-time high level of 47.5 per cent. Notwithstanding the cyclical downturn, yields from direct taxation surged by nearly 19 per cent, boosted by one-off taxes on real estate and bank deposits as well as by receipts from fiscal amnesty. In contrast, the deepening recession slowed the growth of revenue from indirect taxation from 14.5 per cent in 1991 to 5.9 per cent in 1992.

Total **general Government spending**, though rising somewhat less than in 1991 (9.4 per cent compared with 9.8 per cent), reached a peak of more than

57 per cent expressed as a share of GDP (Table 8). The most dynamic expenditure component were interest payments, which surged by nearly 18 per cent, fuelled by rising interest rates and faster debt accumulation. Social transfer payments were boosted by the deepening recession, improved unemployment benefits and the dynamics of pension payments. In contrast, public consumption decelerated, curbed by policies of income restraint. In real terms, the public wage bill contracted by 0.4 per cent in 1992. The rise in subsidies was also held below the rate of inflation, notwithstanding the drop in output, and so was total capital spending, notably investment grants. Thanks to expenditure restraint and sizeable gains in revenues, the budget deficit of **local authorities** was nearly halved to L 5.1 trillion in 1992 (Table 9).

Public debt and debt management

Because of massive deficit overruns in the state budget and currency depreciation, which boosted the lira value of Italy's foreign debt, the public debt position deteriorated sharply. Posting by far the biggest rise in the debt ratio among high-debt OECD countries (nearly 6 per cent of GDP), Italy saw its public

Table 9. **Public sector budget deficits in 1992**

Trillions of lire

State budget deficit[1]	
Old definition	163.1
New definition[2]	159.0
of which:	
Deficit of autonomous companies and other affiliated entities[3]	17.9
General government budget deficit[4]	143.2
of which:	
Local authorities budget deficit	5.1

1. The state sector, *settore statale*, includes the central government, autonomous companies, *aziende autonome*, and other state agencies.
2. Excluding deficits of autonomous companies, the legal status of which was changed to that of a joint-stock company in 1992, *i.e.* state monopolies (MS), state telephone service (ASST) and state railways (FS).
3. *Aziende autonome statali e enti assimilati.*
4. The general government, *amministrazioni pubbliche*, includes central government, local government and social security institutions, but excludes state agencies and some of the other affiliated entities.

Sources: Ministero del Bilancio e della Programmazione Economica (1993), *Relazione generale sulla situazione economica del paese*; Bank of Italy (1993), *Assemblea Generale Ordinaria dei Partecipanti*, Appendice, pp. 122-133.

Diagram 13. **THE PUBLIC DEBT/GDP RATIO AND ITS COMPONENTS**

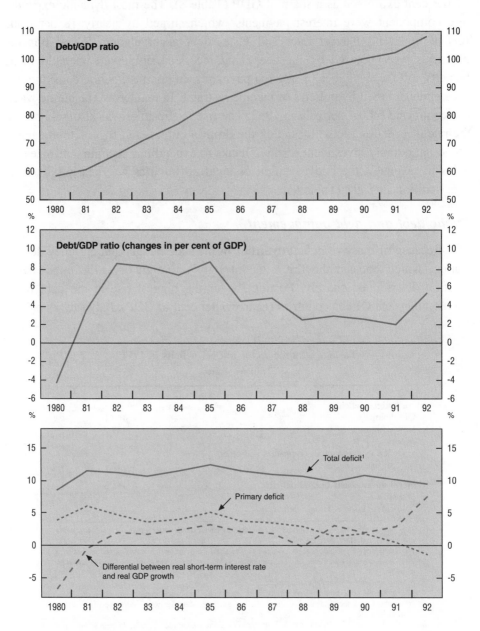

1. General government budgetary deficit in GDP.
Source: OECD, Analytical Data Base.

debt soar to 108 per cent of GDP in 1992 (Diagram 13). Residents hold the bulk (94 per cent) of this debt. Due to a loss in investors' confidence, the share of medium- and long-term securities in the financing of State borrowing requirements shrank to 56 per cent from 75 per cent in 1991, interrupting a trend which began in 1989. Short-term borrowing jumped to 28.5 per cent of state borrowing from 7.6 per cent in 1991, while the relative importance of Postal Savings as a source of loanable funds diminished further (Table 10). Given these relative shifts, the average maturity of the public debt, after peaking at three years and one month in May 1992, began to shorten, declining to two years and ten months in January 1993, rising thereafter to nearly three years in August 1993.

Almost four-fifths of Italy's total public debt in 1992 was accounted for by domestically-issued Government securities, of which 30 per cent in three to 12-month Treasury bills, 28 per cent in fixed-rate medium and long-term bonds and 38 per cent in floating-rate securities with rates tied to the 12-month Treasury bills. The share of foreign issues amounted to less than 4 per cent. With a view to

Table 10. **Financing of State borrowing requirements, 1988-1992**

Percentage shares

	1989	1990	1991	1992
Medium and long-term securities	44.2	48.0	74.8	56.0
Treasury bills	32.2	27.8	7.6	28.5
of which:				
Bank of Italy	−2.2	..	..	..
Bank of Italy financing other than securities purchase	1.4	1.9	1.6	4.4
of which:				
Treasury overdraft facility	1.4	1.9	1.3	4.7
Post office deposits	11.3	8.8	7.7	6.5
Foreign loans	6.4	10.3	3.6	−0.1
Other	4.5	3.2	4.7	4.7
Central government borrowing requirement	100.0	100.0	100.0	100.0
of which:				
Creation of monetary base	4.8	0.5	0.1	..
Central government borrowing requirement (in trillions of lire)[1]	133.8	145.3	152.3	163.1

1. Including settlements of past debts.
Source: Bank of Italy (1993), *Bollettino Economico*, February 1993, p. 22a.

further strengthening the secondary market for Government securities and easing the cost of public debt management, the Government undertook a number of steps. Ten-year futures for Government bonds (BTP) began to be traded on the newly established Italian Futures Market (MIF) in September 1992, about one year after such securities were introduced on the London International Financial Futures Exchange (LIFFE) and the *Marché à Terme International de France* (MATIF).[23] The new market quickly attracted sizeable funds, without, however, reducing the scale of operations on the LIFFE and MATIF.[24] A medium-term futures contract for 3½ to 5 year bonds was introduced in December 1992. In addition, to enhance flexibility of debt management, the Government presented a bill to Parliament in June, authorising the Treasury to issue bonds denominated in foreign currency. In order to promote transparency of debt management, it also intends to draw up a one-year calendar for issues of domestic public debt, setting out amounts and types of regular debt instruments to be issued. Details on issue conditions would be provided every three months.

Budget policy for 1993

The 1993 budget has been widely welcomed as a landmark for it embodied the effects of structural, deficit-reducing measures. Through a Delegation Law, the Government has obtained from Parliament special powers to cut primary spending in four major areas: public employment, pensions, health and local authorities finance.[25] The Delegation Law provides a framework for breaking with the past practice of using one-off measures as a main vehicle of deficit reduction. It is seen as being the main instrument to promote fiscal convergence.

Within the confines of the delegation law, structural reform measures have been taken promptly. The shift towards action yielding budget effects of a more lasting nature was underpinned by institutional changes, curbing Parliament's power to take spending initiatives. As from 1992, spending increases proposed by Parliament have to be balanced by revenue gains. In addition, Parliament's influence over public pay has virtually disappeared, except in a few isolated cases.[26]

Drawn up in September and approved in December 1992, the budget initially envisaged a cut in the deficit from L 163 trillion to L 150 trillion (9.6 per cent of GDP), aiming at a primary surplus of L 50 trillion or 3 per cent of GDP (Table 11). Relative to the estimated deficit on unchanged policies of L 243 tril-

Table 11. **State borrowing requirements in 1993 and 1994 – summary of trend and target values**

	Trend		Target	
	Trillions of lire	Per cent of GDP	Trillions of lire	Per cent of GDP
Outcome 1992[1]	163.1	10.4		
1993 Budget				
September 1992	243.0	15.6	150.0	9.6
Revenue gains[2]			49.5	3.2
Expenditure cuts			43.5	2.8
Total			93.0	6.0
May 1993			155.0	9.9
			(151.0)[2]	
Revenue gains			6.8	
Expenditure cuts			5.6	
Total			12.4	0.8
1994 Budget				
September 1993	182.5	11.0	144.0	8.7
Revenue gains[3]			3.0	
Primary expenditure cuts			28.0	
Savings on interest payments			7.5	
Total			38.5	2.3

1. Based upon old definition of state budget deficit (see Table 9).
2. Based upon new definition of state budget deficit (see Table 9).
3. Excluding proceeds from privatisation.
Source: Data provided by the Italian authorities.

lion, the original budget plan called for a fiscal adjustment of L 93 trillion or nearly 6 per cent of GDP. The deficit cut was to be achieved through structural measures raising tax revenues (L 42.5 trillion), curbing expenditure (L 43.5 trillion) and privatisation (L 7 trillion). On a cyclically adjusted basis, the 1993 budget proposals would lower the deficit by 1¾ per cent of GDP, by far the biggest proposed adjustment among major countries. Underlying the initial budget proposals were projections of a real GDP growth of 1.5 per cent, subsequently lowered to 0.4 per cent, and a moderation of consumer-price inflation to 3.5 per cent, subsequently raised to 4.5 per cent to allow for inflationary effects from the currency depreciation.[27] Renewed fiscal slippage in the first quarter of 1993 prompted the Government to adopt an additional set of restrictive measures, as required under the agreement on the conditional loan from the EC (see below).

In the light of unforeseen cyclical weakness, the Government relaxed the deficit targets for 1993 in May, scaling down the targeted primary surplus to L 31.5 trillion and raising the targeted global State deficit to L 151 trillion (new definition).

On the **tax side**, the initial consolidation measures, projected to yield L 42.5 trillion in 1993, included:

- a revision of personal income tax brackets and a limitation of compensation for fiscal drag (L 8.3 trillion);
- a new municipal tax on buildings (L 8 trillion);
- tighter rules on income from self-employment (L 7 trillion) and non-deductibility of local income taxes (L 7 trillion);
- reduction in tax exemptions and tax expenditure and receipts from fiscal amnesty (L 4 trillion);
- a special tax on companies' net assets (L 5 trillion); and
- harmonisation of VAT rates in compliance with EC rules and increases in train fares and urban telephone fees.

On the **expenditure** side, savings worth L 43.5 trillion were expected to result from structural reform measures in the domain of health services, pension payments, local authority finance and the public labour market. In the **health area**, the Government planned to transform local health units (USLs) into public enterprises (''inter-regional agencies''), to make local authorities and regions liable to finance spending in excess of minimum levels to be guaranteed for the whole country and to allow from 1995 the setting up of an opting-out service. Health spending would also be curbed via restrictions on free health care and higher co-payments for public-health services. To lessen **local authorities**' reliance upon transfers from the central Government, a communal tax on all types of buildings (ICI) was put into effect in January 1993. Regions were also given the right to receive proceeds from the motor vehicle tax in 1993.

Under the **pension reform**, the compulsory retirement age will be gradually raised to 65 years for men and to 60 years for women, a rise by one year every second year beginning in 1993. The reference period for calculating pension rights has been lengthened from five to ten years and the minimum number of years of contribution required to be entitled to pension payments raised from 15 to 20 years.[28] For all new employees, the whole working period will be used to calculate pension rights. The 1993 budget also blocked new entitlements to early

46

retirement benefits (seniority pensions) and suspended the link between nominal wage growth and pensions. Overall, the Delegation Law seeks to stabilise the ratio of pension outlays to GDP at the 1992 level. With effect from January 1993, employees' contributions to the Pension Fund have been raised by 0.3 per cent of gross earnings to 9.99 per cent. At present, pensions make up 42 per cent of current State expenditure and are the largest expenditure item in the budget. The Delegation Law also encourages the creation of private pension schemes (see Part III). Parliament approved a law to this effect in April 1993.

The provisions of the delegation law concerning the **public labour market** are aimed at pruning expenditure for public employees, while promoting efficiency of the civil service. Public pay was virtually frozen until the end of 1993 as a short-run measure. The civil service reform approved by Parliament in February 1993 "privatised" public employment conditions, *i.e.* public sector labour agreements were changed from administrative into civil law. In addition, a special autonomous body separated from the Government has been set up endowed with negotiation powers so as to ensure consistency between pay rises and fiscal consolidation targets. Finally, the civil service reform gave greater responsibilities to public service managers to augment labour mobility, including the right to lay off public employees.

Faced with renewed fiscal slippage caused by flagging economic activity and a lack of privatisation proceeds, the new Government in May introduced additional measures of fiscal restraint, aimed at holding down the deficit to L 151 trillion or 9.7 per cent of GDP.[29] This would correspond to a primary surplus of L 31.5 trillion as required by the EC-loan agreement of January 1993. The fiscal retrenchment of L 12.4 trillion, almost evenly split between revenue gains (L 6.8 trillion) and spending restraint (L 5.6 trillion), combines increases in indirect taxes with transfer cuts. With effect from 1993, the Government has eased restrictions limiting the compensation for fiscal drag. The latest official estimates put the 1993 State budget deficit at L 151 trillion.

Prospects

The new convergence programme

The new convergence programme drawn up in July 1993 implies increased fiscal stringency over the three-year period to 1996. Compared with previous medium-term plans fiscal consolidation targets have been lowered, mainly because of a more realistic assessment of short-run interactions between fiscal restraint and economic growth (Table 12). The new programme sees economic growth firming to 2.4 per cent in 1996, barely enough to stop capacity use from falling further, while inflation ebbs to 2 per cent in 1996. The plan targets a reduction in the State budget deficit to L 106.4 trillion (excluding proceeds from

Table 12. **Medium-term targets**[1]

	1993	1994	1995	1996
Fiscal targets				
(in trillion of lire,				
ratios to GDP in bracket)				
State borrowing requirements				
1991 plan	110.1	97.3		
	(6.7)	(5.5)		
1992 plan	148.2	125.0	87.0	
	(9.2)	(7.4)	(4.9)	
1993 plan	151.2	144.2	127.8	106.4
	(9.7)	(8.7)	(7.4)	(5.8)
Primary surplus				
1991 plan	48.9	64.4		
	(3.0)	(3.7)		
1992 plan	39.2	66.8	105.0	
	(2.4)	(4.0)	(6.0)	
1993 plan	31.5	31.8	46.1	65.5
	(2.0)	(1.9)	(2.7)	(3.6)
Central government debt				
(in per cent of GDP)				
1991 plan	104.4	103.6		
1992 plan	110.9	113.6	113.5	
1993 plan	119.1	121.4	123.3	123.2
Macroeconomic targets				
(percentage changes)				
Real GDP				
1991 plan	3.2	3.5		
1992 plan	1.6	2.4	2.6	
1993 plan		1.6	2.1	2.4
Consumption deflator				
1991 plan	4.0	3.5		
1992 plan	3.5	2.5	2.0	
1993 plan		3.5	2.5	2.0

1. Three-year macroeconomic and budget projections.
Source: Data provided by the Italian authorities.

privatisation) or 5.8 per cent of GDP in 1996. Widening to L 65.5 trillion or 3.6 per cent of GDP in 1996, the primary surplus is sufficient to reverse the rising trend of public debt from 123.3 per cent of GDP in 1995, the first decline since 1980.

The projected deficit reductions are to be achieved through spending cuts, lower interest payments and extra tax revenues from reduced tax evasion, higher indirect tax and social security contribution rates. Areas to be subjected to expenditure restraint include education,[30] a sector marked by an excess supply of teachers, as well as new health care and pension provisions as envisaged under the Delegation Law of 1992. In addition, new practices of public procurement, avoiding corruption and contract rigging, should reduce "overpricing" in the public sector, strengthening the purchasing power of each lira spent on public investment projects (see below). Taken together, the weight of expenditure cuts in deficit reduction is projected to grow with time.

Budget policy for 1994

In line with the medium-term plan of July 1993, the State budget for 1994 targets a reduction in State borrowing requirements to L 144 trillion (8.7 per cent of GDP) from a projected L 151 trillion in 1993. Privatisation revenue has been deliberately excluded from the budget (Table 11). Reaching the deficit target requires a fiscal adjustment of L 38.5 trillion, preventing the State budget on unchanged tax and spending provisions from climbing to L 182.5 trillion or 10.6 per cent of GDP ("trend" deficit). In stark contrast with past budgets, the proposed deficit reduction relies predominantly on economies in primary spending (L 27.2 trillion relative to trend level), resulting from lower transfers to local authorities, public agencies and firms (L 11.2 trillion), reduced State pension payments (L 5.9 trillion),[31] restructuring of public administration and elimination of overpricing for Government contracts[32] (L 4.4 trillion), continued public pay restraint, increased efficiencies in the public labour market (L 2.5 trillion),[33] and stricter controls of health spending (L 3.2 trillion). On the revenue side, a rise in tax payments of L 6.7 trillion is based upon reduced tax expenditure and higher indirect taxes. Direct tax relief (L 2.9 trillion), taking the form of lower advance income tax payments, reduced taxation of imputed rent and stronger compensation for fiscal drag, partly offsets the tax increase.

Together with a **net revenue** gain (L 3.8 trillion), the reduction in primary spending should yield savings on interest payments of L 7.5 trillion, leaving a primary surplus of L 31.8 trillion or 1.9 per cent of GDP. Overall, the fiscal adjustment envisaged for 1994 is much smaller than for 1993, largely a consequence of structural measures taken in 1993. Even without corrective action, the 1994 budget would still post a primary surplus. Underlying the budget proposals are projections of real GDP growth rising to 1.6 per cent in 1994 and consumer-price inflation easing to 3.5 per cent.

The outlook to 1995

Economic Outlook 54 projections were based on the assumption that budget deficit targets will be broadly met in 1994 and 1995, with the Government adopting corrective measures in the event of unforeseen unfavourable developments. Assisted by rising fiscal stringency and income restraint, monetary policy is geared to avoiding a flare-up of inflation caused by the weaker lira since September 1992. Nominal interest rates are projected to fall in tune with German rates, while premia in domestic interest rates are seen to diminish, given expectations of policies becoming more effective in a new institutional environment.

Against this background, output growth may only gradually recover from the trough in 1993, firming in 1994 and in 1995, remaining well below potential output growth. Main forces seen as shaping the revival of output gains include a pick up of private consumption and gross fixed investment, stimulated by a sustained favourable export performance and rising confidence. Held back by low activity levels and decelerating unit labour costs, inflation should continue its downward trend in 1994, easing to around 3 per cent by the end of the projection period.

Given the projected modest pick up of activity, employment may remain virtually flat, causing the rate of unemployment to climb to 11.7 per cent in the second half of 1995. Deepening labour market slack, policies of income restraint and a more flexible system of wage determination are likely to hold nominal wage growth to historically low rates. Even so, real wage gains can be expected to resume from mid-1994 as consumer price increases subside. The gains in external competitiveness should thus be maintained and, together with stronger market growth, should stimulate exports of goods, enlarging the trade surplus to

Table 13. **Short-term projections**

Percentage changes from previous period, s.a.a.r.

	1992	1993	1994	1995	1993		1994		1995	
					I	II	I	II	I	II
Demand and output										
Private consumption	1.8	−1.5	0.7	1.7	−2.7	0.3	0.4	1.5	1.7	2.0
Public consumption	1.1	0.5	0.0	0.3	0.6	−0.5	0.2	0.3	0.3	0.4
Gross fixed investment	−1.4	−7.1	2.5	5.6	−11.3	1.5	2.3	3.8	6.0	6.8
Machinery and equipment	−1.1	−10.5	3.4	6.6	−16.6	2.0	3.6	4.5	6.9	8.0
Construction	−1.8	−3.5	1.6	4.6	−5.6	1.0	1.1	3.0	5.0	5.5
Final domestic demand	1.0	−2.4	0.9	2.3	−4.0	0.4	0.8	1.8	2.3	2.7
Stockbuilding[1]	0.0	−2.8	0.0	0.0	−4.2	0.0	0.0	0.0	0.0	0.0
Total domestic demand	1.0	−5.0	0.9	2.3	−7.9	0.4	0.8	1.8	2.4	2.8
Exports of goods and services	5.0	9.9	7.2	5.5	13.2	6.8	7.5	7.0	5.1	5.0
Imports of goods and services	4.6	−9.5	4.5	5.7	−17.4	3.0	5.0	5.0	5.7	6.5
Foreign balance[1]	−0.1	5.1	0.8	0.0	8.4	1.0	0.7	0.6	−0.1	−0.3
GDP at market prices	0.9	−0.1	1.7	2.3	0.0	1.4	1.5	2.4	2.3	2.4
Industrial production	−0.6	−2.2	2.9	2.9	−1.4	2.6	3.0	3.0	2.8	3.1
Prices										
GDP price deflator	4.7	3.8	4.1	2.9	3.8	3.9	4.6	3.2	3.0	2.5
Private consumption deflator	5.4	4.5	4.1	3.0	4.6	4.3	4.3	3.6	3.0	2.5
Unemployment rate	11.6[2]	10.2	11.1	11.6	9.9	10.6	11.0	11.2	11.5	11.7

	Trillions of lire			
	1992	1993	1994	1995
Balance of payments				
Trade balance	3.1	37.8	50.3	53.7
Current balance	−32.8	6.5	17.6	23.8
As a percentage of GDP	*−2.2*	*0.4*	*1.1*	*1.4*
General government financial balance	−143.2	−151.8	−144.1	−127.9
As a percentage of GDP	*−9.5*	*−9.7*	*−8.7*	*−7.3*

1. As a percentage of GDP in the previous period.
2. Based on old definition.
Source: OECD projections.

about 3 per cent of GDP by 1995. As a result, the current-account surplus may widen to about 1¹/₂ per cent of GDP in 1995.

Economic prospects remain subject to major risks regarding the spending behaviour of private households as well as inflation. Greater job insecurity could stimulate precautionary savings, delaying the revival of private consumption and gross fixed investment. Moreover, depreciation-induced increases in producer and wholesale prices could at some point spill over into consumer-price inflation, further depressing consumption.

III. The drive for privatisation and structural reform

Among major OECD countries, Italy has the highest Government debt and the largest public stake in the business sector. Although the financial position of the Government has suffered from sizeable losses of public enterprises, the value of state property has often been seen as an important counterpart to the rising national debt. At the same time, however, the key role of the state as a producer of goods and marketable services has been increasingly viewed as a source of economic inefficiency and lack of competitiveness. Yet plans to reduce this role by selling off State property have been made only by recent Governments, pressed by the need to meet the challenge of the single EC market, the urgency of fiscal consolidation and the financial crisis of public enterprises.

In 1992, the Amato Government launched a far-reaching privatisation programme, which could provide an important stimulus to the necessary restructuring of industry and the modernisation of the service sector. The plan foresees the sale of several public banks, insurance companies, industrial firms and utilities. Privatisations could contribute significantly to fiscal convergence, directly through public debt redemption but, more importantly, through confidence effects and efficiency gains, reducing interest payments and improving the primary balance in the long run. Public debt reduction and the sale of public assets to private investors would also help to broaden and deepen financial markets, speeding up their integration into world-wide capital markets. Through their impact on the real economy, capital markets and the Government budget, privatisations should damp the underlying rate of inflation and put downward pressure on interest rates, making it easier for Italy to meet the nominal convergence criteria for the EMU. For these reasons, a coherent commitment to the medium-term privatisation plan should be helpful in restoring Italy's credibility abroad.

Recent privatisation efforts have been spurred by the sharp deterioration of the economic and financial position of many state enterprises, the weak state of public finances more generally and the difficulty of redressing these imbalances by traditional state interventions in the face of stringent EC rulings concerning state aid to the business sector. The implementation of the new Government plan will, however, take time. Many state-owned firms need to restructure their balance sheets and are, therefore, not readily marketable. Large-scale placements of shares of public assets may prove difficult given the abundance of profitable and riskless Government securities, which currently absorb around 70 per cent of households' net financial savings. Restructuring and privatisation of public enterprises may also be delayed by the depressed international conjuncture and the simultaneous implementation of privatisation plans by several EC countries. On the other hand, the recent steep decline in interest rates improved prospects for portfolio shifts in favour of equity shares.

The public enterprise sector[34]

In terms of both weight and scope, the Italian public enterprise sector ranks high among OECD countries: major public utilities are all state-owned at the national and, with a few exceptions, local level and direct state holdings in the business sector range from mining and manufacturing to financial and other marketable services. Despite increased reliance on market forces and large-scale privatisations elsewhere in the OECD area, sales of public assets in Italy during the 1980s were sporadic and more than offset by new state acquisitions. The prominent form of state ownership is the joint-stock company, often controlling numerous firms grouped under large conglomerates. Notwithstanding recent reforms, the legal status of many public enterprises is still far from being homogeneous and does not always conform to private sector norms (in terms of certified balance sheets, employment contracts, etc.). In addition, the control structure is often extremely complex and lacks transparency. Many public enterprises have been consistently making losses and have accumulated huge debts in the last decade (see Annex I).

Size and range

In 1987, public enterprises accounted for an estimated 19 per cent of value added, 24 per cent of gross fixed capital formation and 16 per cent of employment of the non-agricultural business sector.[35] Estimated shares of employment, value added and gross fixed capital formation of public enterprises generally exceeded those of other founding members of the EC (Diagram 14). Compared with other EC countries, the presence of Italy's public enterprise sector is strong in nearly all branches of economic activity (Diagram 15). The difference is largest in industry and in finance and insurance, where it is surpassed only by Portugal (Annex Table A8). As in other countries, public enterprises are dominant in energy and mining and in transport and communication, two branches often considered to be "strategic" and characterised by the presence of natural monopolies.

Of the largest Italian firms (ranked according to net sales) the state owns 12 out of the first 20 and over one-third of the first 50 (Annex Table A9).[36] The largest firms are owned in energy and public services, where economies of scale and vertical integration are common. The number of public enterprises and the share of public employment was also large in 1991 in such industrial areas as plant engineering and installation, iron and steel, mechanical engineering and vehicles, chemicals, synthetic fibres, electronics, glass and foodstuffs. In services, state holdings are sizeable in films and advertising, retailing and publishing.

Similarly, a closer look at the finance and insurance sector reveals that the vast majority of financial intermediation is ensured by public credit institutions. Public banks account for about 60 per cent of total employment in the banking sector, 90 per cent of total financial investment and 80 per cent of total deposits (Annex Table A10). The state owns the third and fifth largest insurance companies (ranked according to premia), with state-controlled insurance companies accounting for around 15 per cent of total premia collected in the economy.

The evolution over time of the share of public enterprises in economic activity (as measured by the average of the value added, gross fixed capital formation and employment shares) confirms the atypical position of the Italian state-controlled sector among EC countries (for details about the historical development of Italy's public enterprise sector see Annex I). During the 1980s, the average share remained virtually unchanged, while it was shrinking in most other countries due to large-scale privatisations (Diagram 16). According to panel data, the number of state acquisitions exceeded the number of sales in each year from 1983 to 1992, excepting 1986 (Table 14) and enterprises acquired by the public

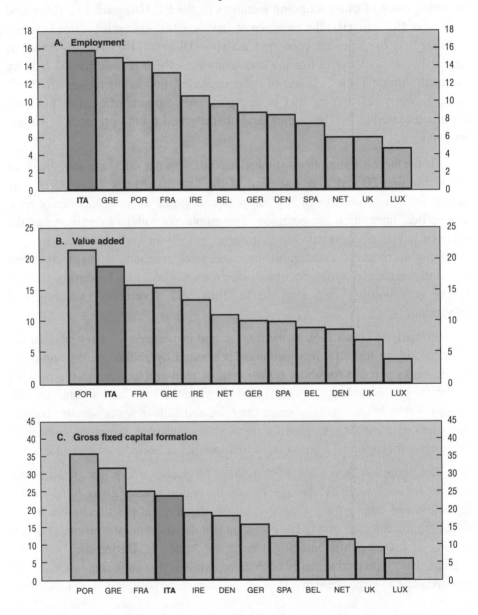

Diagram 14. **WEIGHT OF PUBLIC ENTERPRISES
IN THE NON-AGRICULTURAL BUSINESS SECTOR OF EC COUNTRIES**
Percentage shares in 1987

A. Employment

ITA GRE POR FRA IRE BEL GER DEN SPA NET UK LUX

B. Value added

POR ITA FRA GRE IRE NET GER SPA BEL DEN UK LUX

C. Gross fixed capital formation

POR GRE FRA ITA IRE DEN GER SPA BEL NET UK LUX

Source: CEEP (1990), *L'entreprise publique dans la Communauté européenne: Annales CEEP,* Brussels.

56

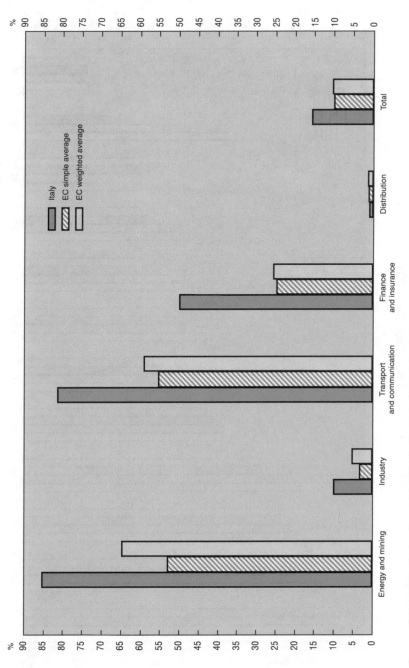

Diagram 15. **EMPLOYMENT SHARE OF PUBLIC ENTERPRISES IN ITALY AND THE EC BY MAIN BRANCHES**

Percentage shares in 1987

Italy
EC simple average
EC weighted average

Source: CEEP (1990), *L'entreprise publique dans la communauté européenne: Annales CEEP,* Brussels.

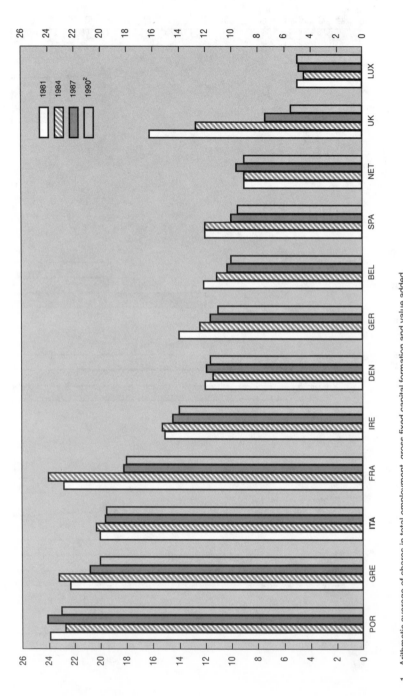

Diagram 16. THE EVOLUTION OF PUBLIC ENTERPRISES
IN THE NON-AGRICULTURAL BUSINESS SECTOR, 1981-1990[1]

1. Arithmetic average of shares in total employment, gross fixed capital formation and value added.
2. Preliminary estimates.
Source: CEEP (1993), *L'entreprise publique dans la Communauté européenne: Annales CEEP*, Brussels.

Table 14. **Acquisitions and sales of public enterprises, 1983-1992**[1]

	A. Over time										
Period	1983	1984	1985	1986	1987	1988	1989	1990	1991	1992[2]	Total
Acquisitions	14	8	17	14	34	22	38	41	28	15	231
Sales	3	5	12	15	16	12	30	20	24	8	195

	B. By size of enterprise[3]				
Staff	> 5 000	> 1 000	> 500	> 100	> 20
Acquisitions	2.5	21.3	37.6	68.9	91.4
Sales	3.7	19.7	33.3	69.1	91.3
Net sales[4]	> 1 000	> 500	> 100	> 50	> 20
Acquisitions	5.3	9.3	37.3	54.7	72
Sales	4.3	5.7	25.7	42.9	70

1. Data refer to transactions of majority stakes between enterprises controlled by private and public owners.
2. First half-year.
3. Cumulative percentage shares.
4. Billion of lira.
Source: Banca Dati, Laboratorio di Politica Industriale-Nomisma.

sector were generally of a larger dimension in terms of both employees and net sales.[37] Over the 1983-1992 period, acquisitions of firms with more than 500 employees amounted to 37.6 per cent of total acquisitions, against 33.3 per cent of firms privatised in the same class. Similarly, acquisitions of firms with net sales exceeding L 100 billion reached 37.3 per cent, against 25.7 per cent of sales of firms belonging to the same class.

Structure and control

In general, state control in Italy takes three main organisational forms: public holdings (*società per azioni*), public agencies (*enti pubblici*) and direct management by a ministry (*aziende autonome*) or a local council (*aziende speciali*). In the early 1990s public holdings became the most widely diffused form of state ownership in industry, services and finance, with either ministries or public holdings being the controlling shareholder (Annex Table A11). Diagram 17 maps the structure of the state enterprise sector before and after recent changes.

Diagram 17a. **CONTROL CHANNELS AND OWNERSHIP LINKAGES:
BEFORE AND AFTER 1992-1993 REFORMS**

A. **Before**

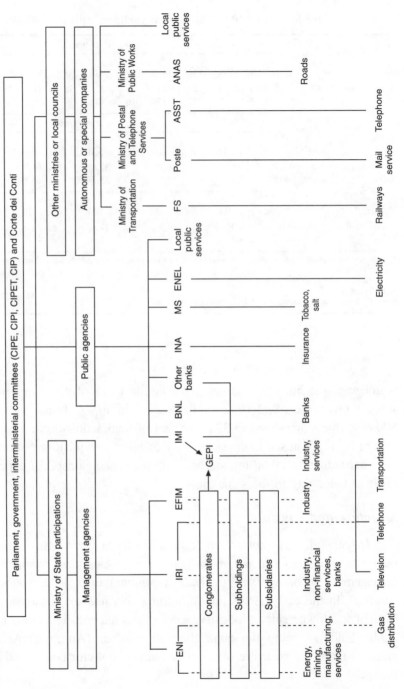

Diagram 17*b*. **CONTROL CHANNELS AND OWNERSHIP LINKAGES:**
BEFORE AND AFTER 1992-1993 REFORMS

B. After

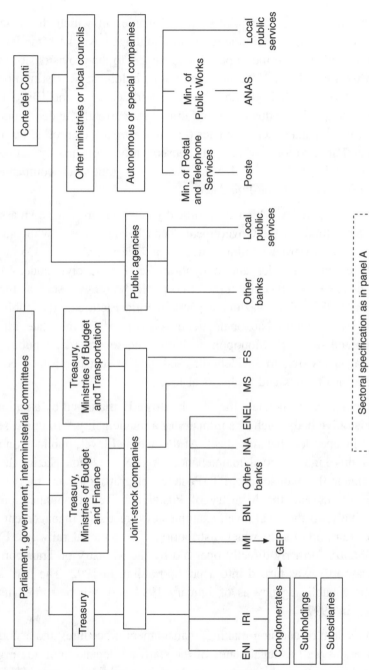

Note: Controls of Corte dei Conti are limited to administrative and legitimacy issues.

Public holdings are joint-stock companies in which the state owns the totality or the majority of shares. Public holdings have the same legal status as private companies and their operation is subject to the provisions of the civil and commercial law. Until 1992, the main public holdings, IRI (Istituto per la Ricostruzione Industriale), ENI (Ente Nazionale Idrocarburi) and EFIM (Ente per il Finanziamento dell'Industria Manifatturiera), currently under liquidation (see below), were management agencies (*enti di gestione*), controlled by the Ministry for State Participations, which was subsequently abolished by national referendum in 1993.[38] IRI and ENI were turned into joint-stock companies in 1992, while EFIM began to be liquidated.

Public agencies, which are juridically autonomous, have own assets, largely endowment funds of the Government. Their balance sheets, while subject to the control of an external administrative or judiciary body (*e.g.* Corte dei Conti), usually escape the rules and obligations set by the civil code. Many public agencies have been recently turned into public holdings – such as the electricity concern, ENEL (Ente Nazionale per l'Energia Elettrica), the public insurance group, INA (Istituto Nazionale delle Assicurazioni), the state monopoly for tobacco and salt, MS (Monopoli di Stato), and several major public banks. But public agencies are still a widely diffused form of state control, especially among financial institutions and at the local level.

Finally, economic activities can be **directly managed** by a national or local administrative body, such as a ministry or a municipality.[39] In this case, the entity has no independent balance sheet. At the national level, public economic activities of this kind are road maintenance, ANAS (Azienda Nazionale Autonoma Strade), and the mail service, PT (Poste e Telegrafi), operated by the Ministry of Public Works and the Ministry of Postal and Telecommunications Services, respectively. At the local level, examples of direct state management range from public transportation to water distribution. The national railways, FS (Ferrovie dello Stato), formerly directly operated by the Ministry of Transport (Ministero dei Trasporti), was turned into a public holding in 1992. The mail service will become a public agency as of January 1994 and will be turned into a public holding in 1997.

Freedom of decision-making, management procedures and accountability of managers as well as legal status of the staff, all depend upon the organisational form taken by the public enterprise. In public holdings, managing directors and the board of directors are appointed by the assembly of shareholders according to the statute of the company, and employees are hired according to private contracts. When the State is the only shareholder, as is often the case, managers are appointed by a political authority, such as a minister or a local council. In addition, strategic and managerial decisions of public holdings have traditionally suffered from the overlap of several layers of control: the political decision level, dispersed over a large number of entities; the management of the holdings, subject to a variety of different statutory rules as well as to political interference; and the management of the controlled subsidiaries. The degree of autonomy of the public conglomerates, as well as the autonomy of subholdings and subsidiaries with respect to the management of the conglomerate, is limited by the inclusion of the conglomerates in the planning legislation, which forces them to present medium-term development programmes to executive and legislative bodies.

Until 1992, political control over the conglomerates was exercised by a number of entities: the Ministry of State Participations, the Inter-ministerial Committee for Industrial Policy (CIPI), the Inter-ministerial Committee for Economic Planning (CIPE), the Government and, lastly, several parliamentary committees all enjoying cross-veto powers. In addition, the board of directors of each of the three conglomerates was composed of a large number of representatives designated by political parties. Recent reforms were aimed at streamlining this control structure (see below). The appointment of managers and the board of directors for public agencies and activities directly run by the public administration is entirely political. In addition, given the special legal status of these bodies, accountability is minimal.

Public conglomerates

The two major public holdings, IRI and ENI, as well as the agency under liquidation, EFIM, are huge conglomerates controlling hundreds of firms employing over half a million people in 1991 or 3.3 per cent of dependent employment. A fourth conglomerate, GEPI (Società di Gestioni e Partecipazioni Industriali), created in 1971, has acted as a "lifeboat" for small- and medium-sized firms in financial trouble, thereby expanding the size of the state in the business sector.

The structure and sectoral scope of the four public conglomerates are shown in Annex Table A12. Their control structure is three-pronged:

- at the top a financial holding, whose board of directors is nominated politically;
- each holding controls a number of sub-holdings, which are generally defined by broad sector of activity and should, in principle, enjoy complete managerial and operational autonomy;
- the sub-holdings have, in turn, a large number of controlled subsidiaries operating on the market in the same way as private firms.

The two major financial holdings, IRI and ENI, are currently controlled by the Treasury, the owner of the totality of their shares. Control by IRI and ENI over the sub-holdings and their controlled subsidiaries is ensured by majority stakes in their equity stock. Minority shares owned by private investors are sometimes significant, such as in the telecommunications and the food and retailing subholdings of IRI (Stet and Sme, respectively) and the electro-mechanical and plant-engineering subholdings of ENI (Nuovo Pignone and Saipem, respectively).

Public financial intermediaries

The credit market is dominated by public agencies, foundations, sub-holdings and limited companies:[40]
- two of the three banks, formerly called banks of national interest (Banche d'Interesse Nazionale), Credito Italiano and Banca Commerciale Italiana, are sub-holdings of IRI;
- the majority of public-law credit institutions (Istituti di Diritto Pubblico), formerly organised as public agencies, were recently turned into state-controlled joint-stock companies as a consequence of the "Amato Law" of 1990; among them, Banca Nazionale del Lavoro (BNL), the only example of an all-purpose bank in Italy, became a financial holding controlled by the Treasury in July 1992;
- most of the special credit institutions (Istituti di Credito Speciale) are public agencies, state-controlled joint-stock companies or public holdings; the largest of them, Crediop, formerly a public agency, became in 1991 a subsidiary of a state-controlled joint-stock company, Banco S. Paolo di Torino;[41] the second largest, IMI (Istituto Mobiliare Italiano), formerly a state-controlled joint-stock company, was turned into a finan-

cial holding controlled by the Treasury in July 1992; others are sub-holdings of IRI and BNL;

- a few ordinary credit banks (Banche di Credito Ordinario) are subsidiaries of IMI and BNL. The vast majority of savings banks (Casse di Risparmio) are state-controlled foundations, public agencies or limited companies.

The state is also widely present in the sector of insurance and financial services. The third largest insurance company, INA (Istituto Nazionale delle Assicurazioni), formerly a public agency, was turned into a public financial holding controlled by the Treasury in July 1992. It ranks second in the area of life insurance and first in the area of all-risks insurance, through its subsidiary Assitalia. Other important insurance companies are subsidiaries of IRI, ENI and IMI. Finally, public holdings also control a number of companies operating in the domain of financial services, leasing and factoring.

Public utilities

All the major public utilities are largely state-controlled either through *de facto* monopoly positions held by public holdings or exclusive state and local concessions to public holdings and agencies.[42] State-controlled public service provision is characterised by a mixture of direct operation through public agencies operating especially at the local level, and public holdings operating in a regime of concession. At the national level, public holdings are becoming predominant after the transformation in 1992 of the public agency for electricity and the autonomous company operating public railways into state-controlled joint-stock companies.[43] The provision of public utilities by function, name, type and ownership of the operating company is shown in Annex Table A13, which also gives information on the market regime and the regulatory framework in which these companies operate and on their market shares in the provision of public services.

With the exception of radio and television, where the private share exceeds 50 per cent of the market, the state dominates public service provision. The public administration has direct control over the mail service and water distribution. Both production and distribution of electricity and gas are dominated by public monopolies, with only partial liberalisations implemented in 1991 in the domain of electricity production and gas transportation. The telephone network is controlled by two sub-holdings of IRI, Stet and the newly-created Iritel,[44] in a regime of exclusive state concessions, except for the market for terminals and value added services, which was liberalised recently in accordance with EC directives. Transportation is also largely controlled by public holdings, operating in a regime of concession. The state concession for rail transportation has been virtually exclusive to date, except for a few minor local lines.[45] Domestic and international air connections are ensured by a sub-holding of IRI, Alitalia (in a regime of non-exclusive state concession), representing 86 per cent of the domestic market for these services. Similarly, the majority of domestic sea cabotage and the highway system are operated by subsidiaries of IRI. Private firms are more present in the areas of waste disposal and local transport, where privatisation efforts were more extensive in the last decade.[46]

The regulatory regime has been characterised by a lack of separation between the regulator and the producer of government services. Exclusive state concessions were generally granted to state-controlled enterprises, whose privatisation was legally impossible until recently.[47] The authority over concession, monitoring and regulation of public services is extremely fragmented. Competences are split among several ministries, local authorities, public companies and national committees,[48] except for the setting of some tariffs, falling under the responsibility of a single Government committee, the Inter-ministerial Committee of Prices (CIP). These entities generally are understaffed and lack a clear focus and mandate.[49] Tariff decisions have often been subordinated to macroeconomic or social policy objectives, such as inflation control or equity considerations: tariffs were kept broadly unchanged in nominal terms from 1962 to 1974 for electricity, from 1974 to 1980 for telephone communications and from 1930 to 1974 for water consumption, causing large operating losses, financed out of state or local budgets.

The privatisation process

Compared to most other OECD countries, Italy is a laggard with respect to privatisations. Some scattered efforts were made during the 1980s (see Annex I) but, as shown above, the number of public enterprises tended to increase even in that period. More systematic efforts were made at the beginning of the 1990s, when a series of legal and administrative measures laid the ground for the more forceful privatisation drive initiated by the Amato and Ciampi Governments. A medium-term privatisation plan, drawn up in November 1992, has begun to be put into effect. At the time of writing, two large companies identified for "immediate" privatisation, IRI's subholding for food and catering, Sme, and the sixth largest Italian bank, Credito Italiano, have been sold to private investors.

Policy and legal foundations

In recent years, a number of Government measures paved the way for a renewed privatisation effort. The main measures were: *i)* the Amato Law of 1990, concerning the transformation of public banks into joint-stock corporations;[50] *ii)* the appointment in the same year of a "commission for the reordering of public holdings and privatisations", known as the Scognamiglio Commission; *iii)* the approval of Law 35 in January 1992, providing the legal basis for privatisations; and *iv)* a law of August 1993 embodying the EC Second Directive on Bank Co-ordination (89/646).

The Amato Law relaxed the state grip on public banks. Although falling short of relinquishing state control over banks, it allowed their transformation into joint-stock companies and the sale of up to 49 per cent of their shares to private investors.[51] The new banking law, which replaces the 1936 Law, legalises universal banking and abolishes the traditional distinction between ordinary and special credit banks, relaxing the constraints on banks' holding shares of industrial companies. Changes in the bank-industry relationship are essential in order to enhance the ability of Italian financial markets to provide the funds needed for large-scale privatisations (see below). A related decree (Decree 481 of December 1992) accords to the Treasury the right to decide on the full privatisation of public banks.

The aims of the Scognamiglio Commission were: *i)* to assess the market value of the public enterprise sector; *ii)* to submit proposals concerning the transformation of public enterprises into joint-stock corporations; and *iii)* to suggest procedures and timetables for the total or partial privatisation of public enterprises. In its final report, presented in November 1990, the Commission made two major suggestions: first, the transformation of public enterprises into joint-stock companies must be seen as a prerequisite for privatisation; and second, success of the privatisation process would be best assured by placing a few large-sized and profitable public enterprises on the market rapidly.[52] The report also set out the main goals to be achieved through privatisations: increase productive efficiency and the degree of market competition, widen the stock market, promote international financial integration and reduce public debt.

The suggestions of the Scognamiglio Commission were partly embodied in Law 35, which provided the legal basis for turning management agencies (IRI, ENI and EFIM), public agencies (such as CREDIOP, IMI and ENEL) and autonomous companies (such as Ferrovie dello Stato and Monopoli di Stato) into joint-stock corporations. It also created the legal basis for the sale of both minority and majority stakes of these corporations. However, the law maintained severe constraints on these operations, since sales of minority stakes were still subject to the approval of an interministerial committee (CIPE) and those of majority stakes to Government and Parliament approval.

The new Government initiatives

In July 1992, the Amato Government liquidated EFIM, the third largest public conglomerate, and announced a far-reaching privatisation plan which broke with the piecemeal approach of the past. These new initiatives largely reflected increasing domestic and international constraints faced by the Italian Government: repeated fiscal slippages in 1991 and 1992 had left no room for continued state support to public enterprises and called for one-off revenues from privatisations; in addition, the more frequent use in recent years of monitoring and legislative power by the EC in the field of relationships between Government and state enterprises has prompted the Government to virtually stop the flow of endowment funds and other forms of State aid;[53] finally, in the absence of assistance from the state, loss-making public conglomerates with ballooning net financial indebtedness were forced to raise resources through asset sales.

The liquidation of EFIM

Decree 487 of July 1992 abolished EFIM, the 45-year old public conglomerate employing about 37 000 people.[54] Liquidation of EFIM had become inevitable given the ballooning stock of outstanding financial debt and the persistently huge losses incurred by the conglomerate, which by 1992 had completely wiped out its own capital. The decree sanctioned *i)* the liquidation of EFIM; *ii)* the immediate assignment to the market of most of its subsidiaries; *iii)* for the purpose of restructuring before sale, the transitory lease of some companies (*e.g.*

those operating in the area of rail transportation and defence) to a subholding of IRI, Finmeccanica; and *iv)* the reimbursement of the majority of EFIM's debt by the state. Though ending the state involvement in a loss-making economic activity, the decree had a series of negative repercussions. The clumsy management of EFIM's liquidation damaged the credibility of the Government, putting pressure on the lira.[55] The reimbursement of EFIM's debt by the State will put a heavy burden on the budget for several years.[56] It also spurred a dispute over State aid with the EC Commission which was resolved in July 1993. Italy is entitled to guarantee the debt of her fully-owned public enterprises in accordance with the Italian civil code. However, the Government is required to reduce its holdings in **all public enterprises** by 1996, thereby putting pressure on the authorities to persist in their privatisation efforts.

The medium-term privatisation plan

In the second half of 1992, prospects for a genuine withdrawal of the state from the business sector were enhanced by two Government initiatives: *i)* Decree 333 of July 1992, later modified by the Parliament and turned into law in August (Law 359), streamlined substantially the procedures for privatisation by changing the legal status of a number of state-owned enterprises and centralising authority over decisions concerning their management; and *ii)* in November 1992, the Treasury presented a comprehensive medium-term privatisation plan as previously announced by the Government.

Law 359 transformed the two remaining public conglomerates (IRI and ENI), the electricity concern (ENEL), the public insurance company (INA) and many public credit institutions, among which the all-purpose bank (BNL) and a special credit bank (IMI) into joint-stock corporations fully owned by the Treasury. This change in status had two main implications. First, their operation and management would henceforth fall under the rules of the civil code.[57] This entrusted their single shareholder, the Treasury, and their managers with the same responsibilities and obligations faced by the owner of a private firm: for instance, civil code provisions would probably have forced the Government to liquidate EFIM much earlier. In addition, their shares can now be listed in the stock market and sold to domestic and foreign investors without parliamentary approval. At the same time, it was decided that future changes in the status of other public enterprises would be sanctioned by CIPE resolutions, rather than by legislative action. Second, partly due to these changes, control over public enterprises was concentrated in the Treasury.[58] The Treasury became fully responsible for appointing managers of the newly-created joint-stock companies, in accordance with their statutes, and was charged with all issues concerning the restructuring and sale of companies as well as with decisions to issue equity and convertible bonds.[59] However, the authority over the privatisation process is shared, since strategic decisions must be taken jointly with the ministries of the Budget and Industry. The Treasury immediately used its new prerogatives to restructure the board of directors of the joint-companies, reducing drastically their size through the dismissal of representatives designated by political parties.[60]

The privatisation process proper started in November 1992 when the Treasury presented to the Government the "Reorganisation Plan of IRI, ENI, IMI, BNL, INA and ENEL."[61] The most important features of the plan were the explicit commitments to: i) sell majority stakes of important public companies, utilities and financial institutions; and ii) provide the management of public enterprises with the necessary incentives to sell, by severely constraining the financial support given by the State. Large flows of endowment funds to IRI and ENI were discontinued and ceilings imposed on their net financial debts, including debt guarantees and commitments (impegni di firma) issued by their wholly-owned subsidiaries (Table 15). More generally, the plan set out the economic goals of privatisation, identified the areas of the public enterprise sector to be privatised and provided broad indications on the timetable, management solutions and sale procedures to be adopted.

According to the plan, privatisation proceeds would serve in the short run mainly to augment the net capital of IRI and ENI and to stop and eventually reverse the deterioration of their financial situation, while ensuring sufficient resources to implement realistic restructuring and development plans (Table 16). In addition, part of the privatisation proceeds – excluding those obtained from the sale of subsidiaries of IRI – were to be used for redemption of public debt. To this end, the creation of a special debt-redemption fund has been proposed, which would clearly draw the line between transitory proceeds from asset sales and the deficit-reducing effects of other structural measures. In the medium run, privatisations should affect both the real economy and financial markets. On the real side, privatisation of public utilities would improve the efficiency of public services, while privatisation of industrial firms would increase the degree of

Table 15. **Risk capital provided to public conglomerates by the State, 1980-1992**

Billions of lire

	1980	1983	1986	1989	1990	1992
Endowment funds						
IRI	2 873	4 022	976	230	488	1 007
ENI	350	1 759	90	120	–	n.a.
EFIM	100	594	400	12	500	n.a.
Other[1]	–	21	55	35	25	n.a.
Total	3 323	6 353	1 415	167	850	1 007
BEI loans[2]						
IRI	–	–	1 105	654	–509	–409
ENI	–	–	340	–	–	n.a.
EFIM	–	–	10	–	–	n.a.
Total	–	–	1 455	765	–	n.a.
Bond issues[2]						
IRI	–	–	1 168	–	–778	–514
ENI	–	–	328	–	–	n.a.
EFIM	–	–	255	–	–	n.a.
Total	–	–	1 750	–	–	n.a.
Total funds						
IRI	2 873	4 022	3 249	884	–799	84
ENI	350	1 759	758	120	–	n.a.
EFIM	100	594	665	12	500	n.a.
Other	–	21	55	35	25	n.a.
Total	3 323	6 353	4 621	932	850	n.a.

1. Inclusive of EAGC, CLP, EAGAT and EAMO.
2. Interest and capital guaranteed by state (changes in stocks).
Sources: Ministero delle Partecipazioni Statali; Ministry of Industry; IRI.

Table 16. **Financial plans of IRI and ENI, 1993-1995**

Billions of lire

	IRI[1]		ENI		
	1993	1994	1993	1994	1995
Financial requirements	7 000	5 000	11 073	13 024	9 036
Sources of funds					
Self-financing	0	0	8 921	10 296	11 660
Privatisation proceeds[2]	7 000	5 000	2 564	4 342	2 262
Borrowing	–1 500	–1 300	–412	–1 614	–4 886
State aid[3]	1 500	1 300	0	0	0
Total	7 000	5 000	11 073	13 024	9 036

1. Provisional data.
2. Includes Lira 1 500 billion of new share issues by ENI and its subsidiaries in the 1994-1995 period.
3. Mostly reimbursements of capital and interest on government-guaranteed debt issued in the 1983-1986 period.
Source: The Treasury (1992), *Libro verde sulle partecipazioni dello stato.*

71

market competition by raising the number of large-sized groups operating in industry from the current six (the two public conglomerates, IRI and ENI, and the four main private holdings, IFI-Fiat, Ferfin-Montedison, CIR-Olivetti and Fininvest) to 10 or 12. On the financial side, privatisations are viewed as a way of increasing the equity stock held by households and increase the inflow of foreign capital.

Two main areas of privatisation are identified in the plan: enterprises that can be sold immediately and enterprises for which a longer delay is required. Among the first are banks, insurance companies and profit-making industrial firms, whose sale is expected to imply no major adjustments in employment levels and territorial location of activities. In this context, the need for a rapid and complete sale of all banks belonging to IRI is explicitly affirmed. Enterprises requiring longer privatisation delays comprise two categories: *i)* natural or *de facto* monopolies and other enterprises operating in a regime of state concession; and *ii)* ailing firms requiring a restructuring process before becoming attractive for private investors.

Monopolies and State concessions require several kinds of interventions prior to sale. In some cases, such as the insurance holding, INA, companies are to be reorganised in order to separate public functions from commercial activities. In other cases, such as telecommunications, activities currently split across several firms are planned to be unified, with some of their services to be liberalised. Finally, all public utilities should be given a clear regulatory framework, especially with respect to tariff-setting.

The plan covers a four-year time horizon to complete the reorganisation and partial privatisation of the public enterprise sector. By that time, the state would have given up firms which suffer from structural crises, firms which are outside the industrial core of IRI and ENI and enterprises for which state control is no longer justified on economic grounds, including major public utilities. However, upon completion of the process, significant minority stakes in many business sector activities would still be maintained by the state, with special powers being retained in areas defined as ''strategic.''[62] These holdings would be managed by a newly-created financial holding (FPP, Finanziaria Pubblica di Partecipazioni), a closed-end fund, whose shares could be quoted on the stock market and in which foreign and domestic institutional investors could participate, albeit in a minority position.

Implementation of the plan

The management of the privatisation process is sketched out only broadly in the reorganisation plan, with many issues left unanswered. In light of later developments, the following pragmatic solutions appear to have been adopted (Diagram 18). A committee of three Ministers – the Treasury Minister and the Ministers of the Budget and Industry – is entrusted with the power of formulating proposals and general guidelines during the privatisation process. Operational decisions are nonetheless delegated to the Treasury, which is the unique share-holder of most public enterprises, while the Prime Minister acts in case of major disagreement in the committee. A privatisation division at the Treasury gives technical support to the privatisation committee on legal and economic issues and liaises with the management of the public enterprises. With a view to making the privatisation process more transparent, a special Advisory Committee (Comitato Permanente di Consulenza Globale e di Garanzia), composed of the Treasury Director and four independent experts, was set up in June 1993 to start within 30 days preparations for the first large privatisations. The Committee was asked

Diagram 18. **MANAGEMENT OF PRIVATISATIONS**

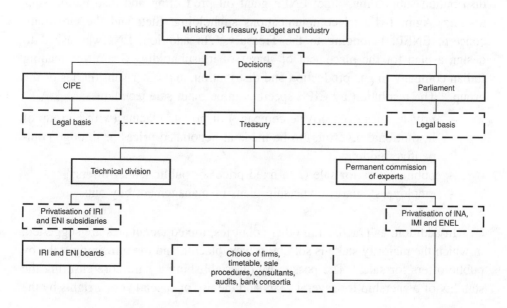

to advise the Treasury on the timetable of privatisation, sale procedures and the choice of evaluation advisers and lead managers for market placements. The management of IRI and ENI is given wide autonomy over the day-to-day conduct of the privatisation and restructuring process of their subholdings and subsidiaries, provided the constraints set by the Government are met (*e.g.* in terms of limits to financial indebtedness and definition of strategic areas).[63] The Government must present an annual report on the state of privatisations to Parliament.

Some other ambiguities of the plan were clarified by the resolutions of Government and the interministerial committee for economic planning (CIPE) of December 1992; the first report of the Government on the state of privatisations, presented to the Parliament in April 1993; and two decrees issued in June and September 1993 by the Ciampi Government. The December resolutions and the two subsequent decrees identified companies to be sold or restructured first, made sale procedures more transparent and specified the special powers to be retained by the Government in "strategic" sectors. Companies to be fully privatised included the fourth and sixth largest Italian banks, Banca Commerciale and Credito Italiano, both belonging to IRI; the special credit bank owned by the Treasury, IMI; the third largest Italian insurance company, INA; a mechanical firm belonging to ENI, Nuovo Pignone; the industrial activities of IRI's food and distribution subholding, Sme; ENI's giant oil production and distribution subholding, Agip; IRI's telecommunications subholding, Stet; and the electricity concern, ENEL, belonging to the Treasury.[64] In addition, ENI was asked to design a plan for the placement of shares of its subholding Snam, the leading Italian company in gas production and distribution, and other subsidiaries of the group.[65] The resolution by CIPE specifies three main sale techniques:

- private sales (to a private company) or private placing (with a group of institutional investors) to be made at negotiated prices or through competitive bidding;
- public offers for sale (at a fixed price) or public tender offers;
- employees' shares ownership plans or management buy-outs.

In addition, as practised in other countries, mixed techniques are suggested, in which the majority stake is sold by private placing and the remaining stake by public offers for sale.[66] The possibility of establishing a hard core ensuring the stability of ownership for several years and the use of special voting rights by the

Government is also envisaged, especially when selling public utilities. The resolution also regulates procedures for the determination of the market price of privatising firms and the design and assessment of restructuring plans, by requiring the contribution of external auditing and consulting firms as well as legal and fiscal experts, and has established rules for the formation of bank placement consortia.[67] An important role in settling all these issues was attributed to the Advisory Committee created by decree in June (see above).

The September decree took concrete steps towards facilitating the sale of major banks, insurance companies and public utilities. While the use of a broad set of sale techniques was reaffirmed, a number of measures waiving or changing Civil Code provisions for public holdings were aimed at making their sale through public offers easier. Statutes were allowed to be changed to ensure a better representation of minority shareholders and to put limits to the amount of shares owned by single partners. Shortly afterwards, the boards of IMI, Credito Italiano and Banca Commerciale changed their statutes accordingly.[68] The decree also summoned public enterprises operating in the areas of defence, transportation, telecommunications and energy to change their statutes in order to provide the Treasury with two main powers: the right to veto the acquisition of large shareholdings by any single agent and to forbid the breaking-up, liquidation or transfer abroad of the company.[69] Once established, these special powers may not be further modified and, most importantly, they only last up to five years. Finally, the decree reaffirms the possibility of placing shares of public holdings by exchanging them against Government securities.

The report of the Amato Government on the state of privatisations and later decisions by the Ciampi Government provided a more precise specification and timetable of ongoing privatisations (Table 17). By December 1993:

- the industrial activities of IRI's food and catering subholding, Sme, had been sold (raising a total L 747 billion) and the sale of the remaining distribution and catering activities was underway;
- EFIM's subholding for glass, Siv, had been sold (raising L 210 billion);
- sales of small ENI-subsidiaries had yielded a total of L 833 billion;
- procedures for the sale of Nuovo Pignone (ENI) and a number of smaller subsidiaries of IRI, ENI and EFIM had reached an advanced stage;

Table 17. **Timetable of privatisation process as of December 1993**

Company	Situation	Measures planned prior to sale and deadlines	Date of privatisation
Sme (IRI)	Broken up into Italgel, Cbd and Sme Italgel sold by private tender (L 437 billion). Cbd sold by private tender (L 310 billion). Different procedures being examined for Sme.	–	1993
Siv (EFIM)	Sold by private sale (L 210 billion).	–	1993
Nuovo Pignone (ENI)	Private tender offers are being examined.	–	1993
Sidermar (IRI), Nuova Italiana Coke (ENI), Unicoke (ENI), Nuova Breda Fucine (EFIM), Breda Energia (EFIM), Ecosafe (EFIM)	Deadline for participation to auction has been announced.	–	1993
Credito Italiano (IRI)	Sold by public offer (L 1 800 billion).	–	1993
IMI	Advisors for valuation and lead-managers for placement have been nominated. Sale of first tranche (20%) by public offer is planned.	–	1994
Banca Commerciale (IRI)	Board of directors of IRI decided full privatisation by public offer. Advisors for valuation and lead-managers for placement have been nominated.	–	1994
INA	Net assets have been evaluated. Break-up of public and private functions has been done. Advisors for valuation and lead-managers for placement have been nominated. Sale by public offer is planned.	–	1994
Ilva (IRI)	Board of directors of IRI endorsed break up of company and full privatisation.	Break-up into three companies. Two of them (including profitable plants and excluding debt) are to be privatised through private sales, the remaining one (including loss-making plants) is to be liquidated. Detailed plan due by October 1993.	–

Stet (IRI)	Reorganisation of telecommunication services approved by government. Services run in regime of concession by several IRI subsidiaries will be unified into Telecom Italia.	New regulatory framework and tariff reorganisation. Advisors for valuation and lead-managers for placement to be nominated by October 1993.	1994 First tranche
ENEL	Advisors for valuation have been nominated.	New concession, tariff and fiscal regime by October 1993. Lead-managers for placement to be nominated by September 1993.	1994
Agip (ENI)	Is being restructured in order to isolate "core business" and get rid of participation in Enichem.	Legal definition of the company and determination of the concession regime. Advisors for valuation and lead-managers for placement to be nominated by September 1993.	1994-95

Source: Data supplied by the Italian authorities.

– are of IRI's largest banks, Credito Italiano, was sold by public offer to domestic and foreign investors, yielding around L 1 800 billion;

– procedures for the sale by public offer of Banca Commerciale Italiana, the other major bank owned by IRI, as well as IMI, the special-credit bank belonging to the Treasury, had begun to be implemented.[70] The sale of Banca Commerciale was planned for February 1994, immediately after the placement of a first tranche of IMI in January 1994;[71]

– the insurance company, INA, was readied for the market and its sale through public offer was planned for summer 1994;

– the EC refusal to allow state aid to the bankrupt iron and steel subholding of IRI, Ilva, prompted its break up into profitable and loss-making plants and financial restructuring in view of full privatisation. A plan was presented to the Commission in October;

– a number of measures were taken in order to prepare the sale of ENEL (the electricity concern) and Stet (the telecommunication subholding of IRI) as well as the energy "core business" of ENI.

In the report on the state of privatisations, the Amato Government announced the creation of four independent regulatory bodies to supervise public services in the domains of energy, telecommunications, transportation and water distribution.[72] In the transition period, tariff policies would be co-ordinated by the Ministry of Industry. In contrast to stated intentions, regulatory reform has not yet started. But, a resolution of the CIPE (April 1993) established the criteria for the reorganisation of telecommunications prior to their privatisation: unification of management of the various relevant IRI subsidiaries; clear distinction between services run in a regime of concession and market competition; and separation of production from service companies. In August 1993, the Government endorsed the above reorganisation plan, and preparations began to create a new company, Telecom Italia, due to be privatised in 1994.[73]

The Government also proposed three laws aimed at facilitating the sale of public enterprises: a draft bill on the expansion of the stock market and laws regulating the creation of private pension funds and closed-end funds, so far absent in Italy (see below).[74]

The economic and financial consequences of the privatisation plan

The main goal of privatisations is to boost economic efficiency. Such gains may derive from stronger market discipline and a strengthening of competitive forces due to both a lower degree of protection and an increase in the number of large groups operating in the market.[75] Up to two-thirds of IRI's industrial workforce and up to 30 per cent of ENI employees produce goods and services in sheltered markets (Table 18). The functioning of financial markets can be enhanced by a wider diffusion and redistribution of shareholdings, which are currently small and excessively concentrated, and as well by the reallocation of

Table 18. **IRI and ENI: Market environment of main non-financial subsidiaries, 1991**

Company	Type of activity	Employment share[1]	Product market regime
	IRI		
Sme	Manufacturing	13.7	Competitive
Stet[2]	Telecommunications/Public service	37.2	Monopoly/Concession
Rai	Telecommunications/Public service	4.4	Concession
Finmeccanica	Manufacturing	15.2	Captive[3]
Alitalia	Transportation	7.9	Concession
Iritecna	Plant engineering	7.7	Captive[3]/Concession
Finmare	Transportation	2.1	Competitive
Ilva	Iron and steel	13.7	Competitive
Fincantieri	Shipbuilding	5.5	Competitive
	ENI		
Agip	Energy	7.3	Competitive
Agip Petroli	Energy	20.0	Competitive
Snam	Energy/Public service	13.8	Concession
Nuovo Pignone	Manufacturing	4.3	Competitive
Snam Progetti	Plant engineering	3.3	Captive[3]
Saipem	Plant engineering	6.3	Captive[3]
Enichem[4]	Manufacturing	28.9	Competitive
Enirisorse	Mining/Metallurgy	7.2	Concession
Enichem agricoltura	Manufacturing	3.4	Competitive
Savio	Manufacturing	1.9	Competitive
Sogedit	Publishing	0.6	Competitive

1. Percentage of total employment of group.
2. Including Finsiel.
3. Predominant public sector orders.
4. Excluding Enichem Agricoltura.
Sources: Ministry of Industry; The Treasury (1992), *Libro verde sulle partecipazioni dello stato.*

portfolios away from huge holdings of public debt. Widening the stock market would improve the ability of firms to raise risk capital. While the Government rightly assigns a lesser role to privatisations for short-run fiscal convergence, in the long term the sale of public enterprises can have important positive effects on the state budget and on public sector net worth.

Privatisations and real activity

A broad indication of potential, direct welfare gains from privatisation can be obtained by comparing the performance of private and public firms. According to aggregate balance sheet data of public and private non-financial firms, public enterprises have been less profitable than their private counterparts over the 1974-1991 period, partly reflecting higher leverage ratios, boosting financial charges, especially in periods of sustained inflation and rising interest rates. But, even in terms of operating surplus, which exclude financial charges (Diagram 19), profitability of public firms has remained inferior except in recent years.[76]

A more differentiated picture emerges when examining the behaviour of firms engaged in the same activity and looking at a wider range of performance indicators. Diagram 20 shows the relative size of profits and labour income as well as labour productivity for public and private firms operating in **competitive markets**.[77] With the exception of electronics and fibres, private firms outperformed public firms in terms of both profits and labour productivity. Their average labour productivity (weighted by sectoral employment shares) was 20 per cent higher in 1991.

Compared with other countries, **public services** are, on the whole, produced less efficiently and have a lower quality (see Table 19 and Annex Tables A1 and A2). The inefficiency of Italian public services is largely attributable to regulatory failure.[78] Technologies, ownership and market structures are similar in most other European countries. The Italian experience shows that the lack of separation between regulatory functions and service production encourages the use of monopoly power rather than the drive for greater efficiency.[79] Even so, Italy has only recently begun to liberalise public service provisions, lagging behind many European countries. Using a combination of privatisation, liberalisation and better regulatory design therefore holds the promise of large efficiency gains.

Diagram 19. **SELECTED INDICATORS OF COMPARATIVE PERFORMANCE OF NON-FINANCIAL FIRMS**

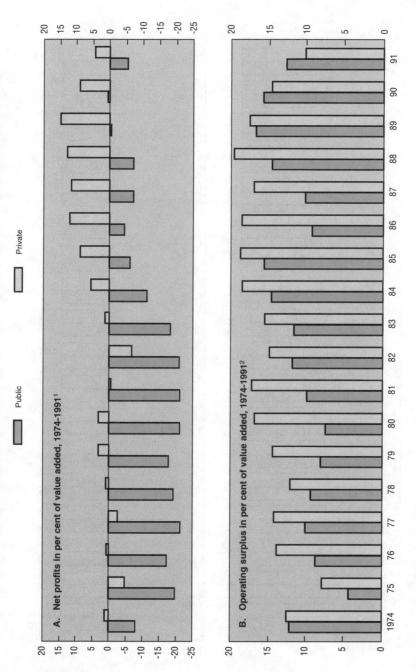

1. Including net interest payments.
2. Net profits excluding interest payments.
Source: Mediobanca (1992), *Dati cumulativi di 1790 societa italiane.*

81

Diagram 19. *(cont'd)* **SELECTED INDICATORS OF COMPARATIVE PERFORMANCE OF NON-FINANCIAL FIRMS**

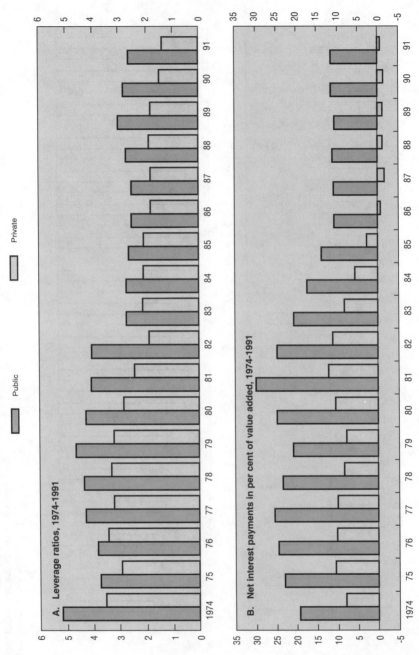

A. Leverage ratios, 1974-1991

B. Net interest payments in per cent of value added, 1974-1991

Public   Private

Source: Mediobanca (1992), *Dati cumulativi di 1790 societa italiane.*

82

Diagram 20. **INDICATORS OF SECTORAL PERFORMANCE, 1991**

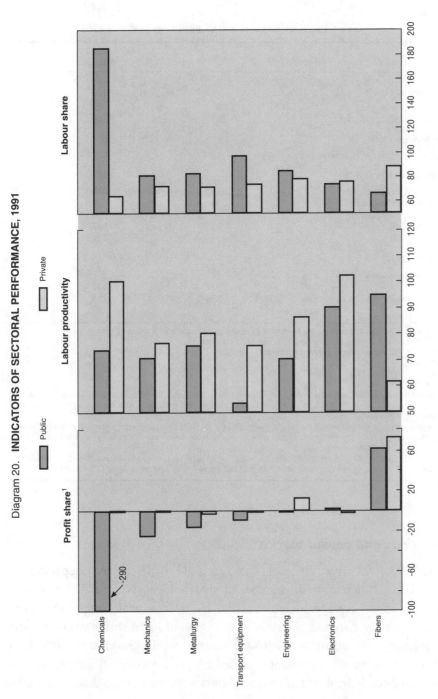

1. Excluding interest payment.
Source: Mediobanca (1992), *Le principali società italiane.*

Table 19. **Costs and prices of public services**

		Italy	Germany	France	United Kingdom	Spain
A. Rail transport (1989)						
Costs per unit of traffic [1]		100	83	50	65	44
Revenues per unit of traffic [1]		100	387	176	243	–
B. Postal services (1988)						
Deficit as a percentage of revenues		39.9	17.3	6.8	–3.4	44.4
C. Telephone services (1991)						
Average cost to households [2]		100	119	86	109	–
Average cost to business [2]		100	84	69	71	–
Difference in cost between calls from and to Italy (%) [3]		–	33.7	14.1	49.7 [4] 78.2 [5]	–20.9
D. Electricity (1992)						
Tariffs for households [6]	min.	123	412	285	325	–
	max.	340	204	203	145	–
Tariffs for industry [6]	min.	200	236	163	155	–
	max.	85	106	76	93	–

1. Traffic units are a weighted average of the number of passenger per km and tons transported per km.
2. For a basket of basic telephone services used by a typical Italian consumer.
3. Maximum tariff for a three-minute call (VAT included).
4. British Telecom.
5. Mercury.
6. Lira per kWh (gross of tax).
   For households. Data for Germany refer to the area of Essen; data for the United Kingdom refer to the area of London. Min corresponds to a capacity of 1.5 kW and an annual consumption of 600 kWh; max to a capacity of 6 kW and to a consumption of 7 500 kWh.
   For industry. Data for Germany refer to the area of Essen; data for the United Kingdom refer to the area of Yorkshire. Min corresponds to a capacity of 100 kW and an annual consumption of 1 600 kWh; max to a capacity of 10 000 kW and to a consumption of 7 000 kWh.
   Sources: Prosperetti, L. (1992), "I servizi di pubblica utilità", *Previsioni dell'economia italiana*, No. 2, Confindustria; Rubino, P. (1993), "Costo e qualità nei servizi pubblici: tre casi", *Competere in Europa*, S. Rossi (ed.).

Privatisations and capital markets

The 1992-1993 privatisation plan also aims at broadening and deepening the stock market and increasing the number of shareholders. While Italian financial markets are about average in relative size by international comparison, their structure is heavily distorted: the ratio of the value of listed shares to GDP is the smallest among the major six OECD countries, while Government securities quoted on the Milan stock exchange exceed 85 per cent of GDP (Table 20). In 1988, shares directly held by Italian households amounted to less than 15 per cent

Table 20. **Comparative size and structure of financial markets, 1990**

Per cent of GDP

	Shares	Debt instruments		Total
		Private	Public	
Tokyo	96.03	4.32	30.65	131
London	87.94	12.87	23.20	124
New York	48.81	5.22	24.97	79
Paris	25.51	7.36	32.14	65
Frankfurt	23.76	34.47	21.77	80
Milan	13.62	6.18	84.20	104

Source: Confindustria (1993), "Risparmio, capitale di rischio e mercato azionario", *Previsioni dell'economia italiana*, No. 1, June.

of GDP, compared to holdings of around 70 per cent of GDP in France and the United States and 40 per cent of GDP in the United Kingdom.[80] Indirect investment in shares, through investment funds or other financial institutions is also relatively small (Diagram 21).

Diagram 21. **COMPOSITION OF FINANCIAL SAVINGS BY HOUSEHOLD, 1991**

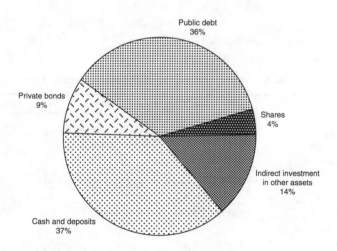

Public debt
36%

Private bonds
9%

Shares
4%

Indirect investment
in other assets
14%

Cash and deposits
37%

Source: Banca d'Italia.

The stock market (concentrated in Milan) is undersized compared to other major OECD countries (Table 21). In 1991, companies listed in the Milan stock exchange (224, of which only two were foreign) were less than a third of those listed in Paris and market capitalisation and annual trade volumes were the lowest among the major six OECD countries. Italian stock-market trade accounted for only 0.8 per cent of the world total against 2.3 per cent for France and 6.1 for the United Kingdom.[81] The weight of public enterprises in the stock market is large. At the end of 1992, the state controlled over 18 per cent of the number of listed enterprises, accounting for over 25 per cent of total market capitalisation.[82] Candidates for privatisation had a share of 18.5 per cent of the total (see Annex Table A14).

The privatisation plan of 1992 foresees the sale of large amounts of shares. In the absence of important institutional investors, these can only be absorbed by increasing the number of small shareholders.[83] Raising L 27 trillion through stock market placements, as envisaged by the 1992 convergence plan, would imply a near-tripling each year of the amount of fresh capital raised in the Milan stock exchange in 1992 (Table 22).[84] Privatising large public utilities (such as Stet or ENEL) necessarily requires a vast diffusion of shareholdings. Notwithstanding initiatives to widen the stock market (discussed in the final section of this chapter), an important contribution to privatisations still needs to come from

Table 21. **Comparative size of the stock market, 1991**

	Tokyo	New York	London	Germany	Paris	Madrid	Milan
Listed companies	1 348	1 885	2 456	667	782	433	224
of which: foreign	125	105	541	239	231	3	2
Average capitalisation of domestic companies/GDP (%)	83.6	54.3	85.8	22.3	25.1	21.3	12.1
Volume of annual trade (US$ billion)	869.7	1 520.2	585.3	432.5	118.8	36.8	26.2
Volume of annual trade of foreign shares (US$ billion)	4.1	88	257.6	8.6	4.1	0.1	0.1

Source: IRS (1993), *Rapporto sul mercato azionario*, Sole 24 Ore.

Table 22. **Fresh capital raised by Italian companies
in the Milan Stock Exchange, 1985-1992**

Billions of lire

	Listed companies	New listings	Total
1985	3 931	824	4 755
1986	14 480	3 743	18 223
1987	5 277	1 532	6 809
1988	3 011	488	3 499
1989	7 355	1 080	8 435
1990	9 408	47	9 455
1991	4 858	247	5 105
1992	3 340	1 457	4 797

Source: IRS (1993), *Rapporto sul mercato azionario,* Sole 24 Ore.

foreign investors, thereby implying an increasing integration of Italy into international financial markets.

Over the medium term, recent innovations (discussed below) could significantly increase the size of indirect investment in equity by households, facilitating the sale of large public firms. The 1992-1993 privatisation plan explicitly mentions the possibility to finance part of privatisations through the voluntary conversion of bank credits to public enterprises into ownership shares. However, for banks to play a constructive role in the privatisation process, two conditions must be met.[85] Being mostly under state control, they need to be privatised first, which, indeed, is the Government's intention; and they need to develop the "know-how" to deal with prospective large participations in industry. So far, the Government has announced the privatisation of three large credit institutions – IMI, Credito Italiano and Banca Commerciale – with Credito Italiano and IMI to be privatised at the turn of 1993 (see above). Judging by the experience of other countries, newly-established pension funds take time before they play a significant role in channelling funds to the stock market.

Given these limitations, a large portion of state assets need to be sold to households and foreign investors, at least over the short run. While the use of special powers by the Government in public utilities and so-called "strategic" sectors (see above) may imply restrictions to foreign ownership, a CIPE resolution emphasises compliance with EC rules. Without increases in households' saving propensities an increase in shareholdings could result either from larger financial savings (to the detriment of households' fixed investment) or from a reallocation of households' portfolios away from public debt and deposits. Larger financial savings could be stimulated by two kinds of measures:

- fiscal incentives to stock market investment, such as those contained in the bill currently under discussion in Parliament, provided these incentives are across-the-board and do not favour shares of privatised firms, otherwise the outcome would be merely to crowd-out resources previously available to private firms;[86] and
- further initiatives aimed at consolidating trust in the correct functioning of the market (e.g. protection of the rights of minority holders, regulation of block trading and bank consortia, enhancement of powers and resources of the supervisory bodies, etc.).[87]

A favourable reception of privatisations by the market requires a credible commitment of the Government and transparent implementation. In this respect, it is important to initiate the privatisation process shortly after the announcement of a detailed programme and to sell the most profitable public enterprises first. As discussed below, transparency requires a clear definition of decisional powers, sale techniques and cases in which special rights may be retained by the state. But the choice of sale techniques has the largest influence in modifying the structure of property rights and financial markets.

The Government has used the private sale technique in the case of Sme and Nuovo Pignone, subholdings of IRI and ENI.[88] However, in order to diffuse ownership rights and increase market discipline over management, public offers will generally be preferred in the future. Given the limited role of institutional investors, resort to fix-price public offers may prove unavoidable. Such offers are bound to be more successful among small savers since this technique is more accessible and the sale price is usually more attractive due to underpricing.[89] In addition, public offers ensure the irreversibility of the privatisation process since a wide diffusion of shares makes it politically difficult for the Government to use special rights or regulatory changes to maintain or recover control of the privatised public utility.[90] Indeed, the public offer technique has been used by the Government in the privatisation of Credito Italiano and has been announced in the privatisation of IMI, INA, and Banca Commerciale, the financial institutions to be sold in 1994, and ENEL, the public utility to be sold in 1995. Measures to make public offers possible have been taken recently (see above). The Government has also decided that banks and small savers will be allowed to convert public debt holdings into equity of privatised enterprises, either by exchanging long-term Government bonds for shares (proposed bill on fiscal incentives and Decree of September 1993) or by purchasing special issues of bonds with warrants (Report by the Government on the State of Privatisations). While failing to increase the size of financial markets, these initiatives would contribute to reduce distortions in portfolio allocation by diverting funds away from Government securities and minimise the risk of crowding out funds otherwise available for private firms. In addition, issues of warrants specifically linked to future privatisations would increase trust in the commitment of current and future Governments to the privatisation plan.

Privatisations and fiscal consolidation

In contrast to previous privatisation initiatives, the new plan assigns only a limited role to one-off proceeds from privatisation in promoting short-term fiscal convergence. Instead, a greater emphasis has been put on improving the efficiency of both the real economy and financial markets.[91] The Ciampi Government even excluded receipts from privatisations as a means for meeting newly-defined fiscal targets for the 1993-1996 period (see Part II). Extraordinary receipts from asset sales cannot per se stop the upward trend of public debt unless accompanied by sustained primary surpluses and a reduction in the effective interest rate on public debt.[92] Even if the totality of public enterprises were to be sold, with all privatisation proceeds used to redeem public debt, the impact on the stock of debt would be limited, since it is estimated that their value amounts to only 15 per cent of public debt (Table 23).[93] On the other hand, given prospective low activity levels and the already excessively high personal income tax ratio, privatisation proceeds may be needed in the short run as a non-deflationary means of limiting public-sector borrowing requirements.

In theory, sales of public assets should leave public net worth unaffected.[94] Nevertheless, there may be positive effects over the longer term on primary balances and debt service. In the case of Italy, these effects may be quite significant:

Table 23. **Estimates of public assets and liabilities**

Billions of lire

	Buildings	Land	Total
Public real estate (1987)			
Central administration	138 807	37 034	175 841
Municipalities	74 885	213 072	287 957
Public enterprises	5 807	150	6 017
Other companies	n.a.	181 229	181 229
Total	219 539	431 485	651 044
Value of major public holdings (1988)[1]		175 600-208 900	
Endowment funds for public enterprises (1990)[2]		245 743	
Public debt (1990)		1 318 356	
Assets in per cent of public debt			
Total public real estate		0.49	
Value of major public holdings		0.13-0.16	
Endowment funds for public enterprises		0.19	

1. Includes only operating companies of IRI whose economic and balance-sheet accounts are reported in the sample of Centrale dei Bilanci.
2. In present value computed using endowment funds from 1930 to 1990 and representative interest rates (discount rate from 1930 to 1947; long-term government bond yield from 1948 to 1972; Treasury-bill yield from 1973 to 1980; interest rate on variable rate government bonds from 1981 to 1990).
Sources: Report of the Cassese Commission (1987); Commissione per il riassetto del patrimonio mobiliare pubblico e per le privatizzazioni (1990), *Rapporto al Ministro del Tesoro.*

– the return from running public enterprises is likely to have been (and remain in the future) well below the cost of servicing public debt.[95] According to the Scognamiglio Commission (1990), the value of state aid financed through borrowing has exceeded the stream of returns expected from this investment. The present value of endowment funds provided by the state since 1930 (around 20 per cent of public debt) has been larger than the current market value of public enterprises (around 15 per cent of public debt).[96] In these conditions, it is certainly profitable for the state to sell its assets, provided it uses the proceeds to redeem public debt rather than to postpone fiscal adjustment. A debt amortization fund (*Fondo di ammortamento del debito pubblico*) was established in November 1993;

- privatisation may also reduce debt service, as interest rates decline on account of improvements in the size and efficiency of financial markets and interest rate differentials *vis-à-vis* international markets. The latter effect stems from lower risk premia (associated with stronger trust in the Italian economy) and lower inflation expectations (associated with reduced expectations of monetisation);
- gains in efficiency linked to improved performance of privatised firms as well as crowding-in of private investment caused by lower interest rates may lead to higher GDP growth, which would permanently increase Government revenues.

On balance, the positive effects of privatisations on public net worth can be expected to outweigh the negative influences. For several decades, public enterprises did not provide dividends to the State, while rents from State concessions were small.[97] On the other hand, privatisations involve transaction costs which are of two kinds: direct expenditures including the cost of advertising the sale of new share issues, fees to accountants, bankers and financial advisors and underwriting fees to financial institutions;[98] and decreases in public net worth due to sale prices likely to be lower than the present value of the future income stream of the privatised public enterprise. This kind of underpricing is likely to occur if:

- private investors have a greater risk aversion than the State (which can pool risks more easily than private agents) and shares are therefore sold at a discount;
- shares are deliberately underpriced in order to attract a large number of investors.

However, the need for deliberate underpricing can be limited by selling equity in instalments. Moreover, underpricing can be reduced if the sales price reflects expected efficiency gains from privatisations.

Problems and limitations of the privatisation process

As noted above, the 1992 privatisation plan and subsequent initiatives by both the Amato and Ciampi Governments provide a consistent framework for substantially reducing the size of the public enterprise sector. A number of unsettled issues, though, could slow down the pace of privatisations: the management and sequencing of privatisations, reform of the regulatory framework for public utilities which are to be privatised, the choice of sale procedures and the scope of the state's planned disengagement.

Management transparency is crucial for the success of privatisations. As it stands, the decision structure adopted in the plan seems overly complicated: three ministries are involved sharing responsibilities in key privatisation issues.[99] The prerogatives of the Government and the boards of IRI and ENI, which are in principle largely independent in the management of privatisations, are not clearly defined. The Treasury division which should provide technical support to privatisations has insufficient staff and resources. Inevitably, this has slowed down the privatisation process, while swiftness in implementing the first sales is important for the credibility of the Government's commitment to the plan. The lack of transparency in the decision structure has been accompanied by repeated changes in the Government's approach to privatisations: the list of public enterprises to be privatised, the privatisation timetable and the planned sale procedures have been changed several times. This has confused potential investors while, at the same time, steps which would have reassured markets, such as the issue of bonds with warrants, have not been taken yet.

The **sequencing** of privatisations has two main facets: what should be privatised first and whether firms should be restructured before their sale. It is clear that the first privatisations will be dictated by the need to restructure the balance sheet of IRI and ENI and to reduce public debt. In setting stringent financial constraints, the Government has implicitly encouraged IRI and ENI to privatise profit-making firms first (*e.g.* Sme and Nuovo Pignone). In pushing ahead with the privatisation of INA and IMI, the Treasury has followed the same approach. The urgency to privatise banks first has increased with the relaxation of the ownership ban for banks (see below). Some public banks have large credits with ailing private firms, such as Ferruzzi, which could be converted into shares under the revised Banking Law.[100] Hence, economic activities subject to public control could even grow during the time banks are not privatised.

Restructuring prior to privatisation may involve legal reorganisation, change in management, rehabilitation or replacement of capital goods, labour-shedding and consolidation of the balance sheet. All these options have either been used or are under consideration. Changes in the structure of the board of directors and in the top management of public enterprises have been extensive since the privatisation plan was announced.[101] Legal reorganisation, including changes in regulation (see below), was imperative for public enterprises operating in a regime of concession (public utilities or enterprises mixing commercial and public functions). A prominent case was the reorganisation of telephone services, bringing several companies under the umbrella of IRI's subholding Stet, to be privatised in 1994-95.[102] In the Government view, capital, labour and financial restructuring are essential for firms hit by structural crisis (*e.g.* chemicals and iron and steel). Some labour restructuring may reduce the social cost of privatisation as well as employees' opposition to it. Reducing leverage ratios and settling arrears may be desirable, especially where it involves a mere cancellation of mutual debts between the Government and public enterprises and among them.[103] In principle, financial and physical restructuring prior to sale presumes that buyers will offer a price which more than compensates the incremental investment by the Government. However, to the extent that ailing public firms can be turned around by restructuring, private buyers would incorporate future efficiency improvements in their valuation of the firm. In this case, the price offered (net of the cost of restructuring) should be the same whether restructuring is carried out by the Government or by the private buyer.[104] In fact, since the Government was unable in the past to ensure the viability of these firms, buyers are likely to offer a price below the cost incurred by the Government. Therefore, postponement of privatisations due to physical and financial restructuring may mask the reluctance of the State to let the market do the job and exposes privatisation proceeds to the risk of being used for cross-subsidising loss-making firms.[105]

The current **regulatory framework**, based on direct management of public utilities or indirect control through IRI and ENI, blurs the relationship between the regulator and the producer, allowing a high degree of monopoly power in the provision of public services. Privatisation of both public utilities (such as ENEL) and IRI and ENI's subholdings (such as Stet and Snam) provides an opportunity to promote competition and improve regulation: public enterprises could be broken up, selling immediately competitive activities; renewal of concessions could be used to liberalise public service provision, while concessions themselves could be attributed with tender mechanisms; and regulatory bodies could be reorganised and reinforced. So far, however, progress in this direction has been exceedingly slow. The Ciampi Government has conferred interim regulatory powers to the Ministry of Industry in several areas, but two main options remain open:

- maintaining the old system, which gives regulatory powers to various ministries including the setting of those tariffs previously set by Government committees (such as CIP);[106]
- creating new regulatory bodies which are authorised to set prices and standards in the domains of telecommunications, energy, water distribution and transportation.

In the first case, staff and resources should be upgraded from currently low levels and steps should be taken to prevent political interference in regulatory decisions. The second solution could ensure a high level of competence, independence and decentralisation in decision-making (thus preventing macroeconomic or distributional factors from influencing regulation); however it would increase bureaucracy, would be more costly and could imply allocation inefficiencies if activities of these new authorities are not well co-ordinated. In both cases, regulatory powers should be circumscribed to tariffs and standards, while the defence and promotion of competition in all areas should be left to the existing antitrust commission. Whatever option is chosen by the Government, decisions should be taken quickly since past privatisation experiences in other countries have shown that a well-defined regulatory framework is essential for maximising both proceeds and welfare gains from privatisations.[107]

The Government has followed a case-by-case approach towards selecting **sale procedures**, favouring private sales and placements until the autumn of 1993. After taking measures facilitating the creation of public companies with broad shareholder bases, the Government announced that it would use public offers in the sale of large public banks. However, a system of market incentives supporting this approach (*e.g.* fiscal incentives to small shareholders, debt-equity swaps, employee shareholding plans) remains to be established. With the first public offers having been made at the turn of the year, such measures are still being examined by Parliament. The Government has yet to clarify whether it will pursue the proposal to issue Government bonds with warrants good for shares of privatised enterprises or whether credits of banks to public enterprises will be converted into shares. It also needs to clarify when and how to stimulate the formation of stable cores of investors, an aim mentioned in several Government documents and decrees. Switching sale procedures also reflects the conflicting aims of widening the stock market, through public offers, generally implying underpricing, and maximising sale proceeds through private sales.

The **scope for state retrenchment** remains undefined. The strategic nature of an activity has been loosely defined in the reordering plan as "the ability to influence outcomes in several other sectors." Although a recent decree circumscribes strategic areas in which the Government will retain special powers, the plan outlines a future industrial structure in which the Government will continue to have significant, albeit generally minority, shareholdings in a long list of activities, including many competitive markets.

The currently depressed economic conjuncture could seriously interfere with a quick implementation of planned privatisations. Due to the recession, many public enterprises to be privatised are at a low point in the earnings cycle and their future profitability is uncertain. Low international activity levels and high interest rates have also reduced the supply of funds available for equity investment. In order for privatisations to proceed speedily, activity and interest rates must return to levels where equity investors can feel confident of economic revival and equities appear attractive compared to bonds. In addition, due to the currency devaluation, the mishandling of the EFIM liquidation and the large credits of banks to heavily indebted public and private firms, Italy's standing on international capital markets had been damaged. Finally, at such difficult times, Italian privatisations must compete with ambitious privatisation programmes of other countries, whose total proceeds are estimated at around $100 billion (Diagram 22). With such an amount of new issuance likely to be placed on the international capital markets, the question arises of whether there is sufficient investor demand on the markets.

Financial market reform

In the past, a number of economic and institutional factors have limited both supply of and demand for equity capital in Italy:

- for more than a decade, the returns on public debt have exceeded the average return on stocks which, over the same period, was more volatile than in other OECD countries; at the same time, capital income taxation heavily penalised returns from equity holdings;
- the role of intermediaries and institutional investors has traditionally been small (up to 1992, only one kind of investment funds, Fondi Comuni, was allowed to operate on the market), while the 1936 banking

Diagram 22. **PLANNED PRIVATISATIONS IN EUROPE**
US$ billion

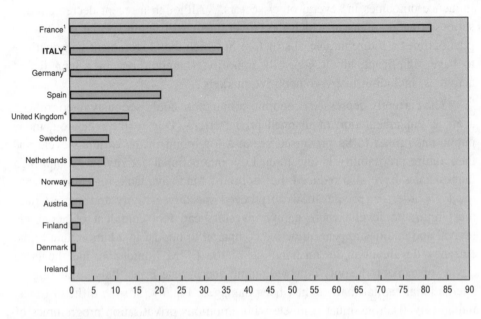

1. Excludes CNP and Bull.
2. Excludes Crediop, IMI, INA, Ilva and Iritecna.
3. Excludes Treuhand.
4. Excludes British coal.
Source: Morgan Stanley Research (June 1993).

law has prevented banks from channelling households' savings towards equity holdings;

– for a number of reasons Italian firms have typically had a low propensity to seek stock market listing and to raise equity capital: prevalence of small individual enterprises, the unwillingness of many medium-sized enterprises to relinquish family control, and strong fiscal disincentives;[108]

– the stock market has only been provided with a modern regulatory framework in the last few years (notably with the 1991-1992 laws on insider trading, take-over bids and the establishment of SIMs) and has suffered so far from lack of transparency, while its supervisory body

(CONSOB) continues to be understaffed of qualified personnel and has little resources and powers.

Over the past three years, several pieces of legislation were passed and other initiatives taken to speed up the **reform of financial markets**, thereby facilitating privatisation (see below):

- the Stock Market Law of January 1991 established a complete legal framework covering the organisation and functioning of the securities markets;[109]
- the SIMs Act of January 1992 created a new type of multi-functional investment firms, incorporated as public limited companies (Società di Intermediazione Mobiliare);
- the establishment of new investment funds (SICAV and others) in 1992 and the creation of closed-end funds in 1993;
- using power under the delegation law of October 1992, the Government laid down the rules governing the creation of voluntary private pension funds in April 1993;
- restrictions banning stakes by banks in non-financial companies were eased in June 1993;
- in January 1993, the Government submitted to Parliament a draft bill on the expansion of the stock market providing fiscal incentives to equity transactions.

The draft bill on the expansion of the stock market:
- sets fiscal incentives to equity transactions which imply loss of majority control of firms, provided the acquired shares are maintained in portfolios for at least three years.[110] Incentives would also be given to the acquisition of shares offered free to the employees of the firms involved in the transactions;
- gives an option for shareholders to pay a 30 per cent withholding tax, instead of declaring dividend income as part of overall income;
- provides an option for Government bond holders to pay for shares of privatised companies with state bonds having a residual life of at least seven years. For payment purposes, the nominal value and not the market value of bonds would apply;

- exempts shareholdings of up to L 100 million from inheritance tax, provided the shares were bought at least a year before the inheritance;
- assigns to the Treasury special shareholding rights (such as golden shares), a novelty in Italian commercial law. These rights include the possibility of appointing representatives in the board of directors, vetoing sales of shares that would lead to loss of control of subsidiaries or subholdings or sales of significant stakes to third parties.

Using powers under the Delegation Law of October 1992, the Government in April 1993 laid down the rules concerning the creation of voluntary **private pension funds**. Open to individuals, professional associations, trade unions and companies, *i.e.* all categories of the labour force except students and housewives, the new funds will be administered directly by the interested parties, subject to investment rules specified by the Treasury, or via conventions concluded with the National Pension Agency (INPS), banks, insurance companies or multi-functional investment firms (SIMs). The three major sources of incomes are regular contributions from employers and employees as well as severance pay (*trattamento di fine rapporto*), subject to a ceiling of 10 per cent of wages.

Employers' contributions to the pension funds can be fully offset against income tax. For employees, tax deductibility is limited to premia up to L 3 million per year. Contributions based on severance pay continue to be tax-free. To ensure budget neutrality, pension fund assets are subject to a wealth tax of 15 per cent, partially reimbursable in the event of pension payments. All pension funds are placed under the surveillance of a special commission composed of thirteen members representing five ministries (Treasury, Finance, Budget, Labour and Industry), the Bank of Italy, the Securities Commission (CONSOB) and ISVAP. As part of efforts to stimulate stock market transactions, CONSOB, using authority conferred on it by the SIM law of January 1992,[111] plans to follow many other countries in introducing a national stock index futures contract.[112]

To broaden the capital market further, the Government Committee on Credit and Savings, following proposals made by the Bank of Italy, eased the **ownership ban for banks** in June 1993. Previous rules forbade banks to own shares of non-financial firms (apart from insurance companies).[113] Limits on the size of shareholding in a given company would be set on the basis of the bank's assets, its structure, profits and management. Under the new rules, banks are permitted to take stakes of as much as 15 per cent of industrial and service firms. A restriction also applies to the amount of funds that each credit institution may invest in shares of non-financial companies. Voted into law in August 1993, the Bank of Italy proposals represent one of the most significant amendments to the landmark 1936 Banking Law. On the basis of the above rules, the banking system could invest up to L 42 trillion (2.5 per cent of GDP) in equity.[114] Given the dominant weight for the moment of State-controlled banks in the banking system, relaxing the ownership ban might simply strengthen the State's influence over the corporate sector, especially at a time of growing debt problems in the private sphere.

IV. Conclusions

Following a protracted period of slow growth, the Italian economy dipped into recession in the closing months of 1992. Output weakness, initially confined to industry, later spread to the service sector. Market sentiment was also affected by the unfolding of corruption scandals involving political parties as well as large public and private companies. The slide into recession would have been steeper had exports not benefited from gains in competitiveness flowing from the lira's sharp fall after September 1992. Judging from conjunctural indicators, the buoyancy of exports may just suffice to keep real GDP in 1993 at its previous year's level, the weakest output performance in nearly 20 years. Massive lay-offs pushed the rate of unemployment above 10 per cent on the new definition in July.

The recent surge in unemployment has been superimposed upon a trend of rising structural unemployment. Absorbing cyclical slack without jeopardising financial stability requires nominal wage growth to remain moderate and regional and sectoral wage differentials to become more responsive to market forces. This, in turn, would create favourable conditions for expanding the employment capacity of the economy. The national labour agreements of 1992 and 1993 have been encouraging developments in this respect.

Rising slack in goods and labour markets together with policies of income restraint led inflation to ease until mid-1993, when the price-raising effects of the currency depreciation began to be felt at the consumer price level. However, at 4.2 per cent in October 1993, the 12-month rate remained almost 1 percentage point below the pre-devaluation level. With a weaker lira and price restraint on the part of foreign suppliers, the trade balance swung into surplus in the second half of 1992, rising to 0.7 per cent of GDP in the first half of 1993. Together with a lower deficit on non-factor services, the better trade performance reduced the deficit on current account to 1.2 per cent of GDP in the first half of 1993. Capital inflows, largely non-bank capital, resumed after the lira's withdrawal from the ERM, strengthening official exchange reserves.

While the lira was forced out of the narrow band of the EMS in September 1992, its subsequent fall on foreign-exchange markets created welcome scope for lowering interest rates. Against a background of falling consumer-price inflation, new measures of fiscal restraint (in May 1993) and greater political stability, the Bank of Italy was able to steer high interest rates gradually down to levels not seen since the mid-1970s. Assisted by a cut in minimum reserve requirements (in February 1993), the excess of the Italian interbank rate over the German equivalent fell to less than 2½ points in September, a level lower than that prevailing prior to the Danish referendum in June 1992. The gap between long-term rates also narrowed. The easing of monetary conditions was accompanied by wide swings in the exchange rate: it fell to historical lows against all major currencies before staging a partial recovery after the referendum on constitutional reform and the formation of a new Government in April.

Faced with an unsustainable public debt position, the authorities have reinforced fiscal restraint. In 1992 there was a budget surplus before interest payments for the first time in over 30 years. On a cyclically-adjusted basis, the overall budget deficit is set to shrink by a total of 3 per cent of GDP over the two years to 1993, by far the biggest fiscal retrenchment in this period among major OECD countries. In particular, the 1993 budget, prepared by the Amato Government, represents a landmark in Italy's recent budget history. It stands out for the weight given to structural deficit-reducing measures, contrasting with the recurrent one-off relief steps taken in the past.

Using special powers obtained from Parliament, the Government began pruning spending in four major areas: public employment, pensions, health care and local authorities' finances. The 1993 budget also reflects efforts to share the tax burden more evenly among different categories of taxpayers. The fight against tax evasion has been stepped up and a minimum tax for the self-employed introduced. Italy's budget plan also became more credible with the EC loan agreement of January 1993, making the staged disbursement of ECU 8 billion conditional upon periodic EC budget reviews. Risk premia in domestic interest rates diminished as a consequence. Finally, public debt management was improved with the creation of a futures market in September 1992.

In spite of the recent progress, the present levels of the general Government deficit and the public debt are extremely high by OECD standards (estimated for 1993 at 9.5 per cent and 114 per cent of GDP, respectively), and the latter is still rising. Thus, fiscal adjustment requirements remain substantial, calling for several years of sustained efforts to meet EC convergence criteria. Difficult as it will be, maintaining the momentum of fiscal consolidation is essential. The scope for revenue gains has narrowed with growing taxpayers' resistance: Italy's income tax rate, including social security contributions paid by employers and employees, ranks highest among OECD countries. The three-year convergence programme of July 1993 has, therefore, been mainly based on spending restraint, involving drastic cuts in primary expenditure. Compared with its predecessors, the programme bears the mark of greater realism regarding the short-run interactions between budgetary savings and economic growth. Counting on both lower interest payments and primary spending restraint via the elimination of pricing abuses in Government contracts as well as reduction in transfers and the public wage bill, State borrowing requirements are envisaged to ease to less than 9 per cent of GDP by 1994 (excluding proceeds from privatisation), before falling below 6 per cent of GDP in 1996.

With greater realism and determination in the pursuit of fiscal targets, as well as an improvement in international competitiveness, the conditions for a sustainable recovery have clearly improved. However, with the expansion of world trade remaining rather subdued, economic growth is projected by the OECD to recover only gradually, with rates staying below potential well into 1995. This would mean that slack in goods and, especially, labour markets may continue to widen. Together with policies of income restraint, firm control of monetary aggregates and greater flexibility in wage bargaining on the basis of the Labour Accord of July 1993, this should keep consumer-price inflation on a downward path, falling to around 3 per cent in 1995. On the external side, the current account deficit may narrow to about 0.5 per cent of GDP in 1995, as both the trade and invisible balance strengthen, in response to the currency depreciation.

Economic prospects remain subject to major risks regarding employment and inflation. Larger employment losses and greater job insecurity could stimulate precautionary savings, delaying the revival of private consumption and gross fixed investment. Moreover, depreciation-induced increases in producer and wholesale prices could at one point spill over into consumer-price inflation, further depressing consumption. Given the downside risks for growth and the operation of automatic stabilisers, it is all the more important to avoid slippage in the reduction of the structural budget deficit. A good budgetary track record is a prerequisite for making Italy's stabilisation programme credible, allowing risk premia in interest rates to ease further, with positive effects on public finance and economic activity.

The projected recovery of economic growth is likely to be accompanied by continuing declines in interest rates, reflecting international developments as well as improved market sentiment about the conduct of fiscal policy. The decline in bank lending rates, on the other hand, may be retarded by the financial crisis engulfing several of Italy's largest private and public firms. The related uncertainties may complicate the already complex task of selling ownership rights in State-owned enterprises. Large in size and exhibiting notorious inefficiency, the public enterprise sector has, for many years, been a drag on productivity growth, notably in the domain of inflation-prone services. The drive for large-scale privatisation, initially motivated by the need to arrest the rapid rise of public debt, is now increasingly seen as a key to improving overall supply conditions. As demonstrated by the superior performance of competing private firms and public utilities abroad, potential welfare gains from privatisation are large. Both the Amato and the Ciampi Governments have taken important measures to roll back the State's presence in the enterprise sector.

The authorities' drive for privatisation rests on four pillars: a new organisational framework within which public enterprises operate (August 1992); a coherent privatisation plan (Amato-Barucci plan), approved by Parliament in December 1992; a set of specific rules speeding up privatisation of all types of public enterprises (decree law September 1993); and new laws and rules aimed at broadening the undersized stock market (pension fund law, draft law on equity investments, and relaxation of the ownership ban for banks). The transformation of all major state-controlled enterprises into joint stock companies with the Treasury as a single shareholder represents a break with the past. It has meant placing debt-ridden public holdings (IRI and ENI), employing half a million people, under the civil code. With Government transfers terminated under EC directives, these holdings are now facing the threat of bankruptcy for the first time. Put under new management, the holdings are now prepared to sell majority stakes of most of their subsidiaries. The State holdings have begun selling profitable companies, with the proceeds being earmarked for restructuring ailing subsidiaries.

In a country long-accustomed to large, *ad hoc* interventions by the public sector, recent Government initiatives represent an ambitious attempt at privatisation. Even so, various factors could limit potential welfare gains: special voting rights in public services and defence have been specified, but the extent of state retrenchment in other sectors remains to be defined; while a broad set of sale techniques has been agreed upon, concrete steps favouring their use (*e.g.* incentive schemes for equity-debt swaps or employees' participation) are still missing; regulatory reform of public utilities has been delayed, retarding privatisation. High priority needs to be given to making privatisation initiatives transparent, especially in a situation where Italy is competing with other countries to attract equity funds. All told, there would seem to be scope for further simplifying the decision-making process, aligning it on that of countries, where progress in privatisation has been more rapid.

The need for setting privatisation targets and specifying methods of implementation is underscored by the recent easing of the ownership ban for share investment by banks in non-financial enterprises. Like the law on private pension funds, this measure was intended to stimulate stock market expansion. Given the likely development of closer ownership links between banks and industry, the Government has rightly stepped up its efforts to sell public banks first. Without such action, the privatisation process could paradoxically go into reverse if banks – most of them still under State control – started converting debt of ailing non-financial firms into equity.

The speed with which political and economic events have been unfolding over the past twelve months or so has surpassed most observers' expectations. Effective steps have been taken to roll back political corruption, which over the years has led to substantial waste of resources. Italy has also given itself a new, majority-based electoral law likely to recast the political landscape. Restoring the credibility of many of Italy's institutions is a prerequisite for lessening deep-seated structural imbalances in goods and labour markets and keeping inflation on a downward course. The authorities' impressive action to make the public debt problem more manageable has been assisted by two parallel developments: the decline in interest rates and improved competitiveness following the lira's departure from the ERM in September 1992 and the labour agreements of July 1992 and 1993. Even so, stabilisation requirements are still large, as demonstrated by the high and rising public debt, huge non-cyclical unemployment and pervasive inefficiencies in the provision of many public services. Dealing with these imbalances and shortcomings requires sustained public support based upon perceptions of equity in sharing the adjustment burden.

Notes and references

1. Panel data for more than 1 800 companies in industry and the service sector show a dramatic drop in consolidated net profits in 1992, caused by spiralling interest payments and depressed revenue growth. Morgan Guaranty Trust Company (1993), *Data Watch: Italy,* 6 August.

2. In October 1992, the Isco indicator of household confidence plunged to its lowest level since the recession of the early 1980s.

3. Disbursements of the Wage Supplementation Fund (Cassa Integrazione Guadagni) have been extended to include large and medium-sized firms in many service sectors. The Fund pays compensation to "temporarily" laid off workers and salaried employees. "Ordinary" recourse applies only to firms in conditions of "temporary" difficulties. Payments by the fund cover 80 per cent of weekly wages based on a 40-hour working week, subject to a ceiling (L 1.2 million in 1993). "Extraordinary" recourse applies to both blue and white-collar workers and involves payments at times of sectoral or local crises or during the process of restructuring of certain industries.

4. Methodological changes included an expansion of the list of branches of economic activity, a more detailed questionnaire and a re-definition of "job-seekers", counting as unemployed persons only those aged more than 15 who were available for work and took at least one initiative to find a job in the 30 days preceding the quarterly labour force survey.

5. OECD (1991), *Economic Survey of Italy,* pp. 50-55.

6. M. Emerson (1988), "Regulation or deregulation of the labour market", *European Economic Review,* Vol. 32, April.

7. Commission of European Community (1993), *5th Report on Employment in Europe.*

8. OECD (1991), *Economic Survey of Italy,* pp. 53-55.

9. In addition, Parliament approved in July a bill raising unemployment benefits from 20 to 25 per cent of the previous wage.

10. The new policy distinguishes between three types of recipients: rural areas, receiving the lowest support; areas hit by industrial weakness; and depressed areas, being accorded the highest assistance. Under new EC rules, depressed areas are those with a per capita income equal to 75 per cent or less of the country average. Into this category fall the following regions: Basilicata, Calabria, Campania, Molise, Puglia, Sardegna and Sicilia.

11. F. Barca and I. Visco (1992), *L'economia italiana nella prospettiva europea: terziario protetto e dinamica dei redditi nominali, Temi di discussione Banca d'Italia,* No. 175.

M. D'Antonio (1992), "Competition, development, inflation: the case of services", *Review of Economic Conditions in Italy,* No. 3 September-December; OECD (1991), *Economic Survey of Italy,* pp. 59-93.

12. Tobacco prices are excluded from the consumer price index.

13. In early April the lira fell to a record low of L 1 002 against the Deutschemark before recovering to L 901 in early June. In mid-September, it stood at L 970 or 23 per cent below the pre-devaluation parity.

14. C.A. Ciampi (1993), "The outlook for monetary policy", statement made before the Budget, Treasury and Planning Committee of the Chamber of Deputies, 20 January.

15. The exemption of non-resident banks' lira deposits from reserve requirements made Eurolira rates more responsive to domestic rates during periods of monetary tightening. Banca d'Italia (1993), *Economic Bulletin,* No. 16, February, p. 39.

16. According to EC regulations differentiation in reserve requirements across different types of deposits can only be based upon maturity considerations. The lower requirement for CDs with longer maturities imposed by the Bank of Italy is thus consistent with EC rules.

17. The adoption of legislation, ending the Treasury's automatic access to central bank credit, provides further scope for the release of blocked liquidity reserves. Under the legislation, the central bank's financial claims against the Government, accumulated under the previous overdraft facility since 1948, would be transformed into Treasury securities to a maximum of L 95 trillion or 6 per cent of GDP, carrying an interest rate of only 1 per cent. However, for purposes of ensuring flexibility in the management of payments and receipts, the Treasury will place with the central bank Treasury bills of at least L 30 trillion at market interest rates. The law explicitly requires the Bank of Italy to suspend payments on behalf of the Treasury if the current balance has been drawn to zero. The law brings Italy into line with Article 104 of the EC Treaty, as modified at Maastricht, which from stage II of EMU precludes the extension of credit or overdrafts by central banks to governments as well as their acquisition of government debt.

18. Repayment of the 12.5 per cent withholding tax on government securities held by non-residents will be speeded up from autumn 1993. Under the new system, depository banks will transmit reimbursement requests directly to the Government, which will automatically send refunds.

19. The ever widening corruption scandal prompted a leading international credit rating agency (Standard and Poor's) to downgrade the rating on Italy's sovereign long-term foreign debt in March 1993. This move followed successive downgradings of Italy's foreign debt by Moody's, another US rating agency, in July 1991 and August 1992. The foreign debt was downgraded from category AA+ to AA.

20. The EC loan is paid in four tranches of ECU 2 billion, of which the first two have been disbursed in 1993. The remaining two tranches will be released in 1994 and 1995.

21. The general government borrowing requirements exclude deficits incurred by autonomous State companies, *aziende autonome statali ed enti assimilati.* The combined deficit of these agencies, which is included in the State budget deficit, more than doubled to 1.1 per cent of GDP in 1992, accounting for much of the rise in the gap between the two measures of budget deficits.

22. For a description of supplementary fiscal measures taken in the course of 1992, see OECD (1992), *Economic Survey of Italy*, p. 45.

23. The short-term future Eurolira contract was launched on the LIFE in May 1992. In June 1992, banking assets in Eurolira totalled L 130 trillion, not far from such holdings in French Eurofranc (L 162 trillion) and Eurosterling (L 182 trillion). See Banca Commerciale Italiana (1993), *The Italian Economy: Selected Issues,* No. 17, January, p. 11.

24. Banca Commerciale Italiana (1993), *op. cit.*

25. The Delegation Law of 22 October 1992 authorises the government to issue legislative decrees, aimed at spending cuts, within predetermined time limits in the four areas cited above.

26. J. de Haan, C.G.M. Sterks and C.A. de Kam (1992), "Towards budget discipline: an economic assessment of the possibilities for reducing national deficits in the run-up to EMU", *EC-Economic Papers,* December, p. 115; J. van Hagen (1992), "Budgetary procedures and fiscal performance", *EC-Economic Papers,* October.

27. Ministero del Bilancio e della Programmazione Economica (1993), *Relazione sull'andamento dell'economia nel 1992 e aggiornamento delle previsioni per il 1993.*

28. The 35-year requirement for receiving a seniority pension from the Pension Agency (INPS) will be extended to all workers.

29. The gap between real interest rates and economic growth widened sharply in the first quarter of 1993, requiring a stronger improvement in the primary balance for any given reduction in borrowing requirements in terms of GDP.

30. The number of teaching personnel, rose by as much as 150 000 persons during the 1980s, largely untenured teachers, pushing up the ratio of teachers to class to levels which are high by international comparison. See A. Monorchio (1992), "The re-qualification of public spending and the control over its principal components: health service, pensions, local authorities, education", *Review of Economic Conditions in Italy,* May-August, pp. 178-183.

31. The proposed measures penalise state employees seeking to leave, as they previously could, after 20 years of work. In addition, pension payments are scaled back for those leaving the state sector before 35 years of service.

32. The budget proposals for 1994 require prices and tariffs paid by the public sector to no longer deviate by more than 20 per cent from prices and tariffs charged in the private sector. Moreover, public procurement contracts will be checked and, possibly, renegotiated in order to bring prices more in line with market conditions. A bill reforming public work rules is awaiting parliamentary approval. The bill aims at reducing heavy overpricing for public work projects caused by corruption and unusually restrictive policies of public procurement. The bill, which establishes a special supervisory agency, also prohibits both contract awards through direct negotiation, rules out price adjustments following the award by drawing a clear line between the planning and execution stages.

33. Pay increases under new contracts in 1994 will be kept below the target rate of inflation. Measures to reform the public labour market include the redeployment of 130 000 civil servants and access of civil servants to the Wage Supplementation Fund.

34. In this chapter the term public enterprise refers to: *a)* enterprises controlled by the state operating in industrial and service sectors; *b)* public financial intermediaries; and *c)* public utilities at the national or local level.

35. CEEP (1990), *L'entreprise publique dans la Communauté économique européenne: Annales CEEP.*

36. Information on a sample of the major 1 898 industrial and service firms is collected and published each year by Mediobanca. Data used in this chapter refers to 1991, Mediobanca (1992), *Le principali società italiane.*

37. For the most recent years, this conclusion is confirmed by the data collected by the Antitrust Commission, which was created in 1990. During its monitoring activity of 1991-1992, the Commission observed 26 public acquisitions of private companies against two sales of state-controlled enterprises to the private sector.

38. The Ministry for State Participations was created in 1956 in an attempt to co-ordinate and supervise more closely the galaxy of public enterprises according to industrial policy objectives. The ministry was never able, however, to accomplish this task and became, instead, one of the major sources of political patronage in the public enterprise sector.

39. Activities can be nested into the administrative unit (*in economia*), or run through so-called Autonomous or Special Companies (*Aziende Autonome o Speciali*).

40. Until 1993, bank legislation divided banks into two broad categories: commercial banks – banks of national interest, public-law credit institutions, ordinary credit banks and savings banks – and the special credit institutions which were allowed to provide medium- and long-term credit, acquire participations in non-financial firms and issue long-term debt. The legal and functional distinctions among the four types of commercial banks and between the latter and the special credit banks have been largely eliminated as a consequence of both the ''Amato Law'' of 1990 and the new Banking Law of 1993 (see below).

41. In 1991, the public-law credit institution Istituto S. Paolo di Torino was changed into a limited company, expanding its activities beyond commercial banking by acquiring Crediop, as permitted by the ''Amato Law'' of 1990.

42. Some public holdings operate in a regime of state concession in areas completely unrelated to public service provision – such as manufacturing and distribution of salt and tobacco, mining and extraction of gas and oil.

43. All stocks of ENEL and Ferrovie dello Stato belong to the Treasury. However, railways are jointly controlled by the Treasury, the Budget and the Ministry of Transportation. The transformation into joint-stock companies of public utilities formerly run as autonomous companies or public agencies implies a change in regime from legal monopoly to state concession.

44. Iritel was created in 1992 to absorb an autonomous company running the inter-city telephone connections Azienda di Stato per i Servizi Telefonici-Asst. The creation of Iritel is part of a wider restructuring effort aimed at bringing telephone services, currently split between Iritel, Sip and Telespazio (two subsidiaries of Stet), under the umbrella of a new sub-holding of IRI to be called Telecom Italia. Restructuring should be completed by 1994.

45. The concession for the construction and management of the high-speed train lines has been granted to a newly-created holding (Tav) in which private capital has a majority stake. Service on these lines will be guaranteed by another holding (Tavco) controlled by the public railways.

46. Subway operation is still confined by law to state-controlled companies.

47. See Cassese S. (1992), "La regolamentazione dei servizi di pubblica utilità in Italia", *L'industria*, No. 2, April-June, pp. 167-173.

48. The most important of these committees is the inter-ministerial committee for economic planning (CIPE), created in 1967, using state-owned enterprises as instruments of industrial policy.

49. For instance, the tariff division of CIP is composed of seven members, of whom only three hold a university degree [Prosperetti L. (1992), "La regolazione delle tariffe dei servizi pubblici italiani: alcune proposte", *Economia Pubblica*, July-August, pp. 343-355, Vol. 10].

50. See OECD (1991) *Economic Survey of Italy*, p. 92.

51. Of the 142 public banks, no fewer than 132 have been transformed into limited liability companies, Fazio A. (1993), "Implications for Italy's banking system of the transposition into Italian law of the Second Banking Directive", *BIS Review*, No. 136, July.

52. The Commission identified five large enterprises for immediate sale: two important special-credit banks, CREDIOP and IMI, the public insurance holding, INA, the electricity concern, ENEL, and the core activities of ENI.

53. The Treaty of Rome defines as *incompatible* state aid to either public or private enterprises, except in specified cases. In recent years the Commission has devoted special attention to public enterprises. In this respect, the key feature of the Treaty is Article 90 that deals with public enterprises and attributes to the Commission the powers of monitoring and address-ing deliberations and directives to member states.

54. In 1962, the Fondo Industria Meccanica (FIM), which had been created in 1947, became EFIM.

55. In 1991, EFIM owed about L 3.5 trillion to foreign banks. Initially, the Government ordered a two-year freeze on the reimbursement of debt, proposing to settle it with long-term government bonds yielding below-market interest rates. Subsequently, the Treasury announced that it would apply to EFIM the rules set by the Civil Code, guaranteeing debt of the holding and of its fully-owned subsidiaries. Repayment of the debt started in May 1993.

56. In addition, the total disengagement of the state from companies formerly belonging to EFIM is not guaranteed. For instance, Finmeccanica has used its pre-emption right over the companies on lease from EFIM to absorb seven defence firms in August 1993.

57. While public agencies are exempt from bankruptcy provisions, the civil code stipulates that a company has either to declare bankruptcy or augment its risk capital if the latter falls below L 200 million. Bond issues, which must be approved by shareholders, cannot exceed the level of capital. In all cases, the unique shareholder has unlimited responsibility and has to guarantee all debt. Hence, the Treasury is accountable for all debts of joint-stock companies with 100 per cent public ownership. This provision applies also to debts acquired before the change in legal status of the public holdings.

58. As part of this reorganisation, the Government proposed the suppression of the Ministry for State Participations. The Ministry was later abolished by national referendum in April 1993.

59. The statutes of the newly-created joint-stock companies generally give the shareholder decisive power in all domains.

60. The board's size was reduced from a range of ten to 20 members to three.

61. The plan was backed by a "Green Book on State Participations", describing the state of the public enterprise sector and analysing issues concerning privatisation (industrial policies, sale procedures, etc.), The Treasury (1992), *Libro verde sulle partecipazioni dello stato,* November.

62. The plan identifies nine sectors were the government plans to keep significant (although generally minority) stakes: electricity; energy and chemicals; banking; insurance; airline transportation; high technology mechanical; distribution and catering; plant engineering and installation; telecommunications.

63. In September 1993 a "Secretariat for Privatisations and Restructuring", headed by an external consultant, was created within IRI to monitor and stimulate privatisations.

64. Except for ENEL and Agip, all these enterprises are listed on Italian stock markets. Both, Credito Italiano and Comit, profitable institutions, have a stake in the merchant bank Mediobanca, which increases their attractiveness (all companies are listed in the London Stock Exchange). Nuovo Pignone has L 450 billion market capitalisation; in addition to making machines and equipment for the oil, energy and textile markets, it controls 9 per cent of the gas turbine market world-wide and has lucrative, long-term co-operation agreements with General Electric Company and the Mitsubishi Group. Sme is a profit-making industrial firm operating in the area of food and catering.

65. Precise plans were requested from IRI for the restructuring of its subholding for iron and steel (Ilva) and its subholding for plant engineering and installation (Iritecna); from EFIM for the restructuring of its subholding for aluminium (Alumix); and from the Ministry of Industry for the restructuring of the public chemical industry.

66. In public offers equity stakes can be sold at different prices and in varying amounts to institutional investors and small shareholders, such as in the "bookbuilt-simultaneous" and "back-end tender" techniques. See Chiri S. and F. Panetta (1993), *Privatizzare: come? Spunti da una ricognizione comparata dei casi inglese e francese, Temi di discussione,* No. 198, Banca d'Italia, for a description of these procedures and their application in the United Kingdom and France.

67. To avoid conflict of interest, the resolution stipulates that evaluation advisers cannot lead placement consortia, but should belong to them as co-managers.

68. In order to speed up the privatisation process, the decree shortens the delays required by the Securities Commission for communicating statutory changes. On the other hand, limits to single shareholdings must be met within three years after their establishment.

69. The companies concerned by these measures will be identified by decree.

70. These procedures include the listing in foreign stock markets, the evaluation of the offer price, the formation of bank consortia and statutory changes, such as upper limits placed on individual shareholdings.

71. Sales of large banks will be staggered over time in order to avoid bottlenecks in the domestic stock market. Attempts to sell IMI and Credito Italiano through private placements were suspended in the course of the year.

72. Regulatory reform is viewed as prerequisite for the privatisation of public utilities, in order to avoid both underpricing due to an uncertain tariff-setting framework and welfare losses due to non-competitive practices.

73. The government intends to privatise first the branch of cellular phones after its liberalisation, which is due by spring 1994.

74. As in some other countries (*e.g.* Chile), private pension funds may become important institutional investors in the stock market, since they are oriented towards long-term financial investments, and could contribute significantly to the success of the privatisation programme in the medium term, Goldstein A. (1993), *Privatizzazioni, fondi pensione e borsa in Cile: un circolo virtuoso?*, *Quaderni dell'Osservatorio sul Mercato Mobiliare*, No. 10, IRS.

75. A World Bank study [World Bank (1992), *Welfare Consequences of Selling Public Enterprises*], concludes that changes in ownership, in both competitive and ''natural monopoly'' markets, have led to sizeable welfare gains in four different countries.

76. Aggregate data are a weak basis for comparisons since they pool production units acting in different markets with different degrees of monopoly power, thereby making it impossible to separate the effects of ownership from those of market structure. In addition, low profitability is not necessarily an index of inefficiency if public firms pursue non-economic goals and are subject to price controls, notably in the domain of public services.

77. See Mediobanca, *op. cit.*

78. Regulation has not been able to meet equity or macroeconomic goals either. For instance, over the 1970-1989 period, the real cost of communication services for Italian households remained unchanged, while it decreased by around 30 per cent in Germany and France. Over the same period, price controls were unable to exert a moderating influence on consumer inflation, Prosperetti L. (1992), *I servizi di pubblica utilità*, in *Previsioni dell'economia italiana*, No. 2, Confindustria, December, pp. 83-125.

79. It is significant in this respect that the most inefficient public utilities, the public mail service and the railways system, are also those in which this confusion has traditionally been largest, since they were directly run as autonomous companies (*aziende autonome*) by the competent ministries.

80. Banca d'Italia (1991), ''La dimensione e lo sviluppo dei mercati finanziari'', *Bollettino Economico*, No. 17, October, pp. 37-49.

81. IRS (1993), *Rapporto sul mercato azionario*, Sole 24Ore.

82. Consob (1993), *Relazione annuale.*

83. British privatisations raised the number of shareholders from 3 to 11 million over the 1981-1991 period.

84. Given the historical record, this is not impossible: in 1986 fresh capital raised was four times as large as a year earlier. However, the current conjuncture is less favourable:

competition between equity and government debt is tighter than in 1986, activity levels are lower and the credibility of the stock market has been shaken by scandals and bankruptcies.

85. See Prodi R. (1992), "Un modello strategico per le privatizzazioni", *il Mulino,* No. 343, pp. 851-861, for a discussion of the potential role of banks in the privatisation process.

86. In France and the United Kingdom the provision of fiscal incentives for equity investment significantly increased households' participation in the stock market, although not all of the increase in direct investment proved to be permanent. See Chiri and Panetta, *op. cit.*

87. See Barca F. (1993), *Allocazione e riallocazione della proprietà e del controllo delle imprese: ostacoli, intermediari, regole, Temi di discussione,* No. 104, Banca d'Italia.

88. Private sales and placings are generally advisable at the initial stages of the privatisation process (since they make it possible to establish quickly the government's commitment to privatisations), when private agreements are sought between the state and the buyer (involving, for instance, stability of ownership control over several years) or when industrial policy aims require a selection of potential buyers (which appears to have been the case for Sme and Nuovo Pignone). These sale procedures are also common when selling enterprises in need of restructuring, since they allow to determine the obligations of the state and the buyer with respect to repayment of debt or employment and production levels. This will probably be the case in the privatisation of Ilva, the iron and steel subholding of IRI.

89. Over the 1979-1987 period, the average underpricing of British privatisations was estimated at 13.5 per cent for fix-price public offers and 11.5 per cent for public tender offers, against an average of 10 per cent in transactions between private investors. The negative conse quences of underpricing for privatisation proceeds can be minimised through fractione sales (see below). Fractioned sales have little impact on credibility, provided loss of st control is obtained during the first instalments. Moreover, French privatisations showed t underpricing is often very small in sales of listed public enterprises, a common situatio Italian privatisations. See Chiri and Panetta, *op. cit.*

90. See Chiri and Panetta *op. cit.*

91. No contribution to the state budget is planned from privatisations made by IRI.

92. Simulations by the Scognamiglio Commission [Commissione per il riassetto del patr mobiliare pubblico e per le privatizzazioni (1990), *Rapporto al Ministro del Tesor* Favero C., G. Keating and J. Wilmot (1992), "Italy: privatisation, the debt ratio and *CSFB Economics,* January, made it clear that even large-scale privatisation plan succeed in stabilising the public debt ratio over a three-year period if the a conditions are not met.

93. A more sizeable contribution to rapid public debt reduction could come from public real estate, whose value is estimated at around 50 per cent of public debt. sales have been planned since 1987, when an *ad hoc* government commissio sione Cassese) produced a report on this subject. However, to date no significa been undertaken, although a real estate intermediation company (Immobiliare trolled by IMI and other public and private banks) has been created to manage tion process.

94. The state exchanges shares of the privatised firms against the capitalised future stream of returns. The private sector foregoes cash and/or financia

these shares. Hence, privatisations only change the composition of public and private portfolios. The fiscal impact of such portfolio changes is unclear. Privatisation and bond issuance (through perpetuities) are equivalent because in both cases the government is accepting to divert future resources from the public to the private sector (the stream of future profits in the case of privatisation and the stream of future interest payments in the case of bond financing). Of course it is crucial that these resources are discounted at the same rate.

95. For a number of years, the real interest rate on government securities has been higher than real GDP growth which, in turn, probably exceeded the average rate of return on public capital.

96. Over the 1947-1990 period, the sum of EFIM's losses has exceeded that of the endowment funds provided by the state, Aronica A. (1992), "Problemi di economicità ed equità nel ritorno al mercato dei gruppi pubblici. La questione EFIM", in *Tentativo di descrizione di un'agenda di governo,* OIKOS. Guaranteed debt to be reimbursed by the state following EFIM's liquidation (L 9 trillion) should be added to this negative balance.

97. Often these rents accrued to individual ministries, making it difficult to quantify their impact on the budget. Public highways (Società Autostrade) pays rents to the state, but the national airline (Alitalia) pays rents to the Transportation Ministry and public television (Rai) to the Ministry of Postal and Telecommunication services (all these companies are subholdings of IRI).

98. Over the 1979-1987 period, the average cost of transactions in British privatisations was between 3 and 5 per cent of gross proceeds (climbing to 7 per cent for public utilities) (see Chiri and Panetta, *op. cit.*).

99. In the United Kingdom and France full responsibility was assigned to a single ministry for each privatisation.

100. The rescue plan for Ferruzzi foresees the contribution of a pool of largely state-controlled banks (San Paolo di Torino, Credito Italiano, Banca Commerciale Italiana, Banca di Roma and Mediobanca), with only a minor role played by foreign institutions.

101. Some of the changes were imposed by the involvement of public managers in the corruption scandals.

102. It is not clear that this choice was optimal in view of the desirable liberalisation of telephone services. Privatisation of Stet (or Telecom Italia) will imply the sale of an (as yet unregulated) monopoly. An alternative would have been to privatise Sip on the one hand and Italcable and Asst on the other, injecting immediately elements of competition in the system. British experience shows that it is easier to liberalise before rather than after privatisation.

103. Financial restructuring, involving injections of fresh capital, was frequent in British privatisations. In some cases, this implied negative net privatisation proceeds (see Chiri and Panetta, *op. cit.*).

104. In some cases, changing the term structure and composition of debt prior to sale may raise the value of the firm.

105. This reluctance as well as the acceptance of the risks may be motivated by fears of the social cost of privatisation, industrial policy aims and the wish to avoid private sale procedures (the only ones appropriate in the case of loss-making or heavily-indebted firms).

106. A bill accompanying the 1994 budget law envisages the suppression of several government committees, among which CIP.

107. See World Bank, *op. cit.*

108. The number of medium-sized firms satisfying the criteria for stock market listing is much larger than the number of firms actually listed [Confindustria (1993), *Previsioni dell'economia italiana,* No. 1, June].

109. See OECD (1991), *Economic Survey of Italy,* p. 93.

110. Each fiscal year, a maximum 27 per cent tax relief is ensured for purchases up to L 7.5 million. The total yearly tax relief cannot exceed L 10 million.

111. OECD (1992), *Economic Survey of Italy,* p. 66.

112. National stock index futures contracts began to be traded by three US futures exchanges in 1982, followed by the United Kingdom (1984), Japan (1986), France (1988) and Germany (1990).

113. From 1990, banks are allowed to buy stakes in insurance companies. Special credit institutions, which conduct medium- and longer-term business, were always free to make such purchases. OECD (1991), *Economic Survey of Italy,* p. 88.

114. See Fazio, *op. cit.*

Annex I

Italy's public enterprise sector: an historical review

The build-up of the public enterprise sector

The clustering of public enterprises in conglomerates operating in a number of areas is peculiar to the **Italian "model" of state ownership**, which was conceived and developed as a safety net for ailing private banks and industries, rather than being the outcome of an explicit industrial policy design. The main public conglomerate, IRI, was created in 1933 in order to avoid collapse of the financial system. It initially performed the role of a financial holding, taking over temporarily the three major all-purpose banks and their stakes in industrial firms irrespective of their economic performance. Ownership was supposed to return to the private sector once the crisis was over. In the event, three years later the holding was made permanent and expanded throughout the post-war period, reaching its maximum size in the 1970s, when it was used again as a lifeboat for firms hit by adverse shocks. Similarly, EFIM, the conglomerate currently being liqui- dated, which took over in 1962 the activities of the state-owned Fondo Industria Manifat- turiera set up in 1947, acted as a channel to provide government financial resources to ailing manufacturing firms in need of fresh capital. The creation in 1953 of the oil and gas conglomerate, ENI, had stronger industrial policy motivations. It was aimed at promoting production, refinement, sale and distribution of oil and gas according to public policy criteria. As a result, it preserved for a long time a high degree of integration. Only recently did its activities transcend its original sphere. Finally, the smallest conglomerate, GEPI, was created in 1971 – with capital provided by the three other conglomerates and a public bank, IMI – in order to take over private companies experiencing temporary difficulties and turn them back to the private sector after reorganisation. In practice, as was the case for many of the firms absorbed by the public enterprise sector, the large majority of these firms remained under its control, using up increasing public financial resources because of their economic difficulties.[1]

In the post-war period, the main **historical roots** of massive state intervention in the business sector were:

- the presence, until the mid-1960s, of sizeable public current account savings, which made resources available for public capital formation;
- the underdevelopment of financial markets, which limited the ability of firms to raise funds directly from households;

- the rigid separation between bank and industry under the 1936 Banking Law, which prevented ordinary banks from acquiring shares and extending long-term credit; and
- the lack of integration in international capital markets.

With institutional impediments limiting the supply of risk capital to private entrepreneurs, the state took direct control over large sections of the economy, providing the necessary financial intermediation so as to ensure an adequate level of overall capital formation.[2] The case for state intervention weakened with the passage of time. Public dissavings now absorb about three fourth of households' savings, and the latter have also been declining steadily. Although the market for risk capital remains undersized compared with many other European countries, financial markets have developed swiftly and are now fully-integrated at the international level. Finally, bank legislation introduced in recent years has profoundly modified bank-industry relationships by allowing financial intermediaries to decrease their degree of functional specialisation. As a result, financial intermediaries and the growing stock market now appear to be capable of channelling (long-term) funds from households to the enterprise sector.

Public enterprises and economic performance

The case for privatisation rests mainly on the notion, now widely accepted, that in competitive markets, private ownership is superior in meeting both the goal of productive efficiency, *i.e.* minimisation of the costs of production, and allocative efficiency, *i.e.* equalisation of marginal costs to prices. In addition, due to changes in technologies used to produce and distribute many public services, the need for public ownership in so-called "natural monopolies" has decreased over time. Therefore, privatisation must be seen as an important means to strengthening Italy's competitive position at a time of rapidly integrating EC markets.

Productive inefficiencies of public enterprises relative to privately-owned firms usually result from differences in corporate control and monitoring and in goals and incentives given to management. In private firms, interests of shareholders, creditors, managers and workers may diverge, but in public enterprises *the problem of control* is compounded by a more complex hierarchy of principal-agent relationships involving the additional interests of politicians and bureaucrats, while taxpayers – *i.e.* the ultimate shareholders – are stripped of most powers.[3] As discussed above, the control structure of Italian public enterprises is particularly intricate due to the overlap of several decision-making levels, including a large number of legislative and managerial bodies, all subject to strong political interference.

Monitoring performance is also more difficult in public enterprises. In principle, in competitive markets, the value and prospects of both public and private firms can be established through movements in their share prices which may vary continuously, reflecting changes in both general market conditions and features specific to the firms. However, only a small number of Italian public enterprises is listed in the domestic stock market, and even fewer are listed in international markets (see below). Possible alternatives appropriate for unquoted public enterprises, such as frequently revised current-cost valuation, are more complex and less accurate than stock market valuation and hinge on the production of reliable accounts by the public enterprises.[4] In Italy, huge public conglomerates such as IRI and EFIM did not provide consolidated balance sheets until the mid-1970s.[5]

Public enterprises have been assigned multiple, often non-economic, goals varying over time with political and administrative changes.[6] Since the 1950s, the government has used public enterprises as an instrument of industrial and macroeconomic policies, in particular for supporting "strategic" sectors and promoting regional development.[7] State-owned enterprises played an important role in the development of the steel and energy industries in the post-war period by ensuring sufficient capital formation and an adequate level of orders through vertical and horizontal integration.[8] But the conglomerates extended their activities well beyond the borders of the above-mentioned strategic sectors and the "strategic" motivation has often been used to justify the acquisition or to prevent the sale of enterprises in any sector of economic activity.[9]

As for *regional development,* a 1957 law imposed on the public conglomerates the constraint of directing 60 per cent of new investment in the country's Southern regions or more if the total share of fixed assets was less than 40 per cent. This policy had, at best, mixed results. In a few areas, constraints to capital formation were removed, especially in the 1960s, and local industrial poles were created. However, industrial activities were often concentrated in sectors later hit by structural crises (*e.g.* steel and chemicals); and in the face of severe labour-market rigidities, capital-intensive sectors were preferred. More-over, the legislative constraints had an important bearing on the increase in overall borrowing requirements of the public conglomerates, resulting in rising transfers through the state budget.[10] Even so, the gap between the Centre-North and the South has been increasing in the last decade, casting serious doubts on the conduct of regional development policies.[11] *Macroeconomic goals* imposed on the management of the public conglomerates included the improvement of the trade balance, the support of employment levels and inflation moderation:

- Balance-of-payments considerations encompassed the development of domestic steel and energy industries in the 1950s and discouraged privatisation of state-controlled food and retail distribution companies, disregarding both economic theory and empirical evidence that protection of domestic markets can, at best, strengthen the foreign trade balance in the short run, with increasingly negative effects over the longer run.
- Employment has been supported by the public enterprise sector, especially in the last two decades. As a consequence, since 1970 employment growth has been stronger in public than in private enterprises in each year except 1978 (Annex Diagram A1).[12] This not only imposed a heavy burden on public conglomerates but also proved to be an inefficient means of employment protection. Indeed, it was estimated some time before the actual liquidation of EFIM that providing social subsidies to the 37 000 EFIM employees would have been less costly for the state budget than continuing financial support to the loss-making public conglomerate.[13]
- In the attempt to moderate inflation, some state-owned enterprises – notably those operating in the domain of public services – have been subject to price controls, especially during the 1970s (see above). This had serious consequences for their

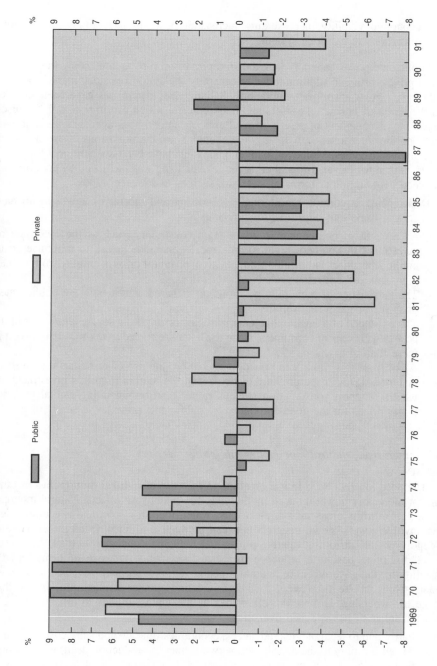

Diagram A1. **EMPLOYMENT CHANGES IN PUBLIC AND PRIVATE ENTERPRISES, 1969-1991**

Source: Mediobanca (1992), *Dati cumulativi di 1790 societa italiane.*

economic viability, necessitating increasing flows of state funds and creating distortions in the price system.

Public enterprises generally lack the *structure of incentives* influencing the management of private firms. In addition to being generally sheltered from stock market monitoring through regular share price quotations, Italian public enterprises have been shielded from the threat of hostile take-overs and bankruptcies, which can impose a fierce discipline on the management of private firms. Public or autonomous agencies, the dominant form of public enterprises until 1992, were exempt from the provisions of the civil code regulating bankruptcies. Moreover, budget constraints have been less stringent for public enterprises than for private firms: their access to financing was facilitated by government-guaranteed debt and other forms of state aid, such as endowment funds.[14]

Deficiencies in control, monitoring, goal-setting and incentives are likely to have translated into important *allocative inefficiencies*:

- As a result of non-economic goals, legal constraints (such as the 1957 law on investment in Southern regions) and, more generally, failure to minimise costs, public enterprises have had a tendency to over-invest or over-employ, so that their input mix did not reflect relative factor prices.
- The persistence of monopoly positions or sheltered activities in the public enterprise sector generates welfare losses.[15]
- The existence of a huge public enterprise sector implies a severe restriction in the portfolio choices of consumers, since the latter are forced as tax-payers to invest in these illiquid assets.
- Apart from this rigidity in portfolio allocation, the use of resources may also be distorted if, under the pressure of taxpayers, the returns from this investment are used to support consumption streams rather than remunerating capital (*e.g.* via lower prices for the goods produced by public enterprises).

Public enterprises, natural monopolies and public services

The need to privatise is less compelling in the case of **natural monopolies** or other forms of monopoly power induced by the presence of network effects. Natural monopolies, in public utility areas such as electricity, water, mail, transport and telecommunications, involve a well-known trade-off between productive efficiency and the exercise of monopoly power, distorting relative prices and reducing consumer welfare. Moreover, market discipline has little influence in these cases, since the size of firms and the possibility for the government of retaining special veto powers after privatisation, *e.g.* via golden shares, make take-overs unlikely. Injecting greater competition, rather than change in ownership, is therefore often seen as the main stimulus to efficiency.[16] The room for doing so has widened over time:

- Partly due to technological advances, economies of scale and sunk costs appear to be related more to the distribution network than to production itself, be it production of a good – as in the case of electricity or water – or of a service – as in transportation, mail or telecommunications. Therefore, competitive forces may be strengthened by breaking up public utilities, with both production and the access to the distribution network being liberalised.[17]

- In many cases, technological innovations have invalidated economies of scope as justification for public provision of services. This is true, for instance, for some mail and telecommunications services.[18]
- In some cases, the removal of barriers to entry and the ensuing market contestability may improve internal economic efficiency of the public utilities, although contestability may not prove sufficient or credible enough to eliminate monopoly power.
- To a certain extent, competition for the market in the form of franchising can be a substitute for direct state control and a valid supplement to regulation of certain public services.

In principle, combining privatisation and liberalisation should improve economic efficiency relative to direct state ownership. In practice though, it may not always be possible to achieve the optimal combination due to the difficulty of sequencing reforms and to political and macroeconomic constraints on the process of privatisation. In addition, as discussed below, welfare gains from privatisation and liberalisation are closely dependent on the design of the regulatory framework.

Italy's provision of public services has suffered from notorious inefficiencies. Both direct efficiency measures and quality indicators identify postal services and rail transportation as the worst-run public utilities (Annex Table A1). The efficiency gap between Italy and other OECD countries is particularly large in cost and tariff levels. In 1989, the cost per unit of traffic of public railways was between 20 and 50 per cent higher than in comparable other OECD countries, while revenues were between two and four times lower. Similarly, the deficit of the Italian public postal service reached 40 per cent of revenues in 1988, far above those of the United Kingdom, France and Germany. Moreover, electricity prices were much out of line with those charged elsewhere (Annex Diagram A2), while telephone calls were much more expensive, especially business and international calls. Over the 1980-1988 period the cost of communication services relative to manufacturing prices increased by an estimated 11 per cent, while falling by 26 per cent in France and 33 per cent in Germany. Over the same period, the cost of transportation services relative to manufacturing prices increased by 37 per cent in Italy, while remaining stable in France and Germany.[19]

Up to the late 1980s, the greater part of these differences can be ascribed to sluggish labour productivity growth, except for electricity where productivity developments were broadly in line with other OECD countries (Annex Table A2). Over the 1970-1988 period, labour productivity fell by an estimated 15 per cent relative to manufacturing in communication services and by 50 per cent in transportation services.[20] Over the same period, relative productivity in communications had increased by 60 per cent and 95 per cent in Germany and France, respectively, while productivity in transportation fell by only 10 to 15 per cent in these countries.[21] Inefficiencies in the service sector are widely held responsible for structural inflation and losses of competitiveness during the 1980s.[22]

Diagram A2. **ELECTRICITY TARIFFS**[1]

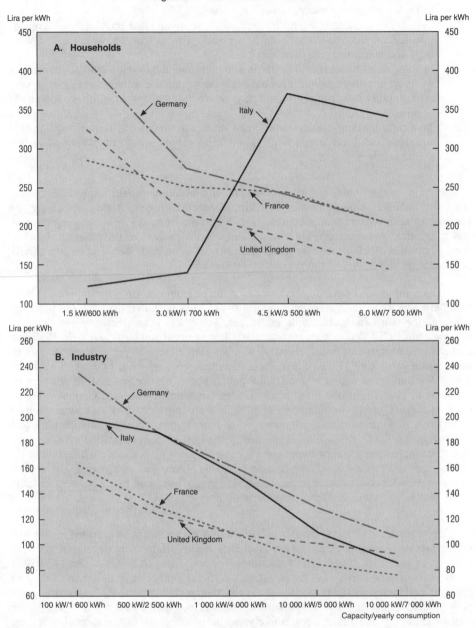

1. Gross of tax.
Source: Prosperetti (1992), "I servizi di pubblica utilità", *Previsioni dell'economia italiana,* No. 2, Confindustria.

Financial evolution of the main public enterprises

Over the last two decades, the financial situation of **public conglomerates** has been rather uncomfortable. Until after the second oil shock, non-economic goals were put above corporate policy considerations: public enterprises were used to preserve and generate jobs, maintain high investment levels and rescue ailing private sector firms, while tariff and pricing policies were often aimed at damping inflation. Towards the end of the 1970s, when rapidly rising borrowing requirements threatened the system with collapse, a process of financial consolidation was initiated assisted by huge government transfers, privatisations and labour-saving measures. Over the 1982-1986 period, government transfers averaged L 5.3 trillion per year (over 0.7 per cent of average GDP) against an average of L 1.8 trillion in the 1978-1981 period. They consisted mainly of endowment funds, supplemented after 1984 by government-guaranteed bond issues and loans by the European Investment Bank. Transfers dropped dramatically in the 1987-1990 period, averaging L 1.2 trillion per year (0.1 per cent of GDP) and virtually ended more recently.

Towards the end of the 1980s, the financial position of public conglomerates deteriorated again, notably for EFIM and the industrial section of IRI (Annex Table A3). Despite restructuring efforts, EFIM continued to make losses: by 1991, its net financial debt surpassed L 8 trillion, almost twice the value of its net sales and over half per cent of GDP.[23] The industrial section of IRI, after a temporary improvement from 1988 to 1990, also recorded net losses and net financial charges at the end of 1992 amounting to 6 and 9 cent of net sales, respectively, pushing net financial debt to about 90 per cent of net sales (5 per cent of GDP). In 1993, a re-evaluation of the conglomerate's assets by the government, involving a transformation of government-guaranteed debt into own capital, and accelerated reimbursement of tax credits avoided financial collapse. The deterioration of the financial situation of the oil and gas conglomerate, ENI, and of the electricity concern, ENEL, was less serious.

The consolidated accounts of IRI and ENI mask wide differences between financial situations of their **subsidiaries**. Loss-making subsidiaries included plant engineering, sea transportation, iron and steel and shipbuilding for IRI and mining, manufacturing and publishing for ENI (Annex Table A4). Most of these areas have been suffering from long-standing structural crises and only survived because of sustained support from profitable subholdings, such as the telecommunications subsidiary of IRI and the oil and gas subsidiaries of ENI.

The financial results of **public credit institutions** have been generally good (Annex Table A5). With the exception of Banca Nazionale del Lavoro (BNL), whose accounts suffer from both excessively high operating costs and creation of reserves needed to meet possible loan defaults,[24] both ordinary and special credit banks displayed in 1991 sizeable net profits, large intermediation margins and high capital/asset ratios. However, since public banks have been providing the virtual totality of credit to public enterprises (Annex Table A6), their financial soundness is closely linked to the economic performance of the public enterprise system.

The privatisation experience of the 1980s

In contrast to the widespread tendency of state-retrenchment in the OECD area, only a few large privatisations were made in Italy in the last decade and not all have implied a genuine loss of control by the state. Generally, privatisation was seen as a source of funds for restructuring public conglomerates or a way to internationalise ownership of public banks, rather than a means of reducing the role and size of the public enterprise sector.[25,26] Partial privatisations involving sales of minority holdings or decrease in majority holdings by the state were frequent, but only rarely did they bring about change in ownership or control of industrial firms or credit institutions. Overall, the amounts raised through full and partial privatisations were small as compared to privatisation proceeds in other OECD countries. However, for IRI and ENI the contribution of full and partial privatisations to the process of financial consolidation has been significant (Annex Table 7).[27]

Several procedures have been used in the privatisation process. In full privatisations, subsidiaries of the main public conglomerates were generally sold through private sales rather than market placements. Often, these sales were preceded by a period of industrial restructuring.[28] In partial privatisations, placements on the stock market, through either new listings or sale of shares previously held in the portfolios of the public holdings, usually took the form of syndicated or tender offers.[29] Finally, fresh capital was also raised through the issue of convertible bonds and bonds with warrants. The issue of these financial instruments was often found to be more attractive for investors and less costly for the state than the issue of debt or equity.

In manufacturing, the main privatisations concerned Alfa Romeo (1986), a loss-making firm whose sale to FIAT yielded over L 1 trillion to IRI in 1987;[30] Lanerossi (1987), whose sale to Marzotto marked the exit of ENI from the textile sector; Sopal food processing (sold by EFIM in 1990); and the sale of the diesel engine subsidiary by IRI, and SIR fine chemicals (sold in 1987). Apart from a few small banks, the only important privatisations in the area of credit concerned Mediobanca (1987) and Crediop (1991), two of the largest special credit institutions. Even after the sale of Mediobanca shares by the three IRI-controlled "banks of national interest" (Banco di Roma, Banca Commerciale and Credito Italiano) the state p reserved a stake of 25 per cent in the bank, with the remaining shares subdivided between a stable core of Italian and foreign investors (25 per cent) and a number of smaller shareholders (50 per cent). On the other hand, the majority stake of Crediop was sold to the Istituto S. Paolo di Torino, after the transformation of the latter into a state-controlled joint-stock corporation. Protracted negotiations between the Treasury and a group of state-controlled Casse di Risparmio for selling a majority stake of IMI, the state-owned special credit institution, definitely broke down in 1993.

The sale of Mediobanca and Crediop were important initiatives in the context of the restructuring of the financial market aimed at the development of universal banking and the ending of the rigid separation between commercial banking and industry. In the event, however, none of these transactions had involved complete loss of control by the state: IRI's shareholdings in Mediobanca are still sizeable compared to the stakes of any other private investor and Crediop was sold to a state-controlled credit institution.[31]

The privatisation episodes of the 1980s highlight the potential problems caused by the lack of coherent guidelines, procedures and goals ruling the privatisation process. They also revealed the dispersion of decisional powers concerning sales and acquisitions of enterprises by public conglomerates. In contrast to what happened in other EC countries, where privatisations were promoted by the government, sales of subsidiaries of the public conglomerates were initiated by their managers and often met with stiff resistance from government and legislative bodies. For instance, the agreement reached by IRI to sell its food-processing and retail distribution subholding, Sme, was stalled and finally cancelled in 1985, due to both political interference and alleged lack of transparency in the bidding procedure.[32] In 1986, the government appointed a special commission (Commissione Varrone) to clarify the respective roles of management and state in the sale and acquisition of enterprises. The commission concluded that subholdings of the public conglomerates should enjoy complete autonomy in small-sized non-strategic transactions, while political approval would be required for strategic operations (*e.g.* involving the disengagement from specific sectors of activity) or operations implying revisions to the medium-term programmes presented to the parliament. Given the ambiguity surrounding the notions of both strategic operations and revisions to medium-term programmes, the conclusions of the commission left largely unaffected the leverage of political power on the financial and industrial policy decisions of the conglomerates.

Notes and references

1. For more details on the history of the public conglomerates, see:
   - Coltorti, F. (1990), "Phases of Italian industrial development and the relationship between the public and private sectors", *Rivista di politica economica,* No. V, May;
   - Maraffi, M. (1990), *Politica ed economia in Italia,* il Mulino, Bologna;
   - Momigliano, F. (1986), *Le leggi della politica industriale in Italia,* il Mulino, Bologna; and
   - Bottiglieri, B. (1984), "Linee interpretative del dibattito sulle partecipazioni statali nel secondo dopoguerra", *Economia pubblica,* No. 4-5, April-May, pp. 239-244.

2. On the other hand, the configuration of credit markets resulting from state intervention may have contributed to the underdevelopment of the Italian stock market. See Trento, S. (1993), "Il gruppo d'imprese come modello di controllo nei paesi ritardatari", *Temi di discussione,* No. 196, Banca d'Italia, May.

3. Bureaucrats may want to maximise the size of their department as well as their costs of operation. Politicians may want to maximise chances of remaining in office, by offering patronage and servicing their constituencies.

4. These alternative procedures inevitably reflect the techniques and subjective views of the sponsoring ministry or regulator rather than the subjective views of a variety of agents with different degrees of knowledge and attitudes towards risk. In addition, the management of a private firm has an incentive to provide information about its performance, since the threat of acquisition deters it from undervaluing its assets, while the management of a public enterprise may be tempted to bolster its monopoly power by retaining and using more information about itself than is available to government departments, let alone customers and suppliers.

5. EFIM was required by law to issue a consolidated balance sheet from 1972 onwards, while IRI did not make such figures available until 1974. In addition, the absence of standard accounting principles rendered these data virtually meaningless (see Coltorti, *op. cit.*).

6. Profit-making has been discouraged since it is technically difficult to distribute dividends to the government. Resources have thus been used to make new investments or repay borrowings. Moreover, if the politicians' goal is to maximise political support, there will be a tendency to make no excess profits, since these will be rather distributed as wages or rents to constituencies.

7. It is open to question whether direct state control of economic activities rather than incentive schemes or structural reforms are needed to ensure the development of strategic sectors or depressed regions, even at early stages of development.

8. See Maraffi, *op. cit.*

9. Resistance to the privatisation of IRI's food and catering subholding has often been justified by qualifying these activities as strategic.

10. World Bank (1988), *Techniques of Privatisation of State-owned Enterprises,* Vol. II, Technical Paper No. 89.

11. In 1992, Agensud, the agency for the development of the South, was closed.

12. Public employment policies were clearly countercyclical at the beginning of the 1970s, in the aftermath of the two oil crises and during the 1982-1983 recession. The data underlying Annex Diagram A1 refers to a sample comprising the major 1 198 public and private enterprises (see Mediobanca (1992), *Dati cumulativi di 1 790 societa italiane*). The sample contains always the same set of firms, *i.e.* it is "closed" over time. Therefore, changes in ownership of large firms are reflected in employment growth differentials. This explains the outlying observations of 1987-1988, two years in which large privatisations were made (notably Alfa Romeo), and the swing of 1989, probably reflecting the nationalisation of Enimont.

13. Aronica, A. (1992), "Problemi di economicità ed equità nel ritorno al mercato dei gruppi pubblici. La questione EFIM", in *Tentativo di descrizione di un'agenda di governo,* OIKOS. Similarly, losses from continuing operations of the public-owned coal mines in Sardinia (Carbosulcis) are estimated to be much higher than any social protection scheme for its 400 employees; The Treasury (1992), *Libro verde sulle partecipazioni dello stato.*

14. Debt guarantees imply that external, internal and financial disciplines in public enterprises are insufficient incentives to induce profit-seeking behaviour. Such guarantees undermine management discipline.

15. Little attention has been devoted to the control of monopoly power of public enterprises or to fair trading between public firms as well as between public firms and private suppliers. When the state is regulator, shareholder and client separation of interests is likely to be blurred.

16. However, even in the case of natural monopolies, change in ownership may have a positive effect on efficiency since: *i)* regulation is more effective than ministerial control; and *ii)* the process of privatisation requires a fundamental re-thinking of the internal organisation of the firm, which leads to the suppression of slack resources.

17. Breaking up is advantageous whenever the resulting stimulus to efficiency stands to exceed the loss of economies of scale or scope. These considerations motivated the Open Network Provision by the EC.

18. The directives of the EC imposing liberalisation in the domain of specialised mail services and value-added phone services sanction this state of affairs.

19. Prosperetti, L. (1992), "I servizi di pubblica utilità", *Previsioni dell'economia italiana,* No. 2, Confindustria, Rome, pp. 83-125.

20. In more recent years, labour shedding has significantly improved labour productivity in Italian public railways. In 1991, traffic per employee increased by a record 13.9 per cent.

21. Prosperetti, L. (1992), *op. cit.*

22. Barca, F. and I. Visco (1992), "L'economia italiana nella prospettiva europea: terziario protetto e dinamica dei redditi nominali", *Temi di discussione,* No. 175, Banca d'Italia. Over the 1976-1990 period, the price of services relative to non-energy products increased by 28 per cent in Italy and by less than 14 per cent in France and Germany (Prosperetti, L. (1992),

"Efficienza e qualità nei principali servizi di pubblica utilità: l'Italia nel contesto internazionale", *L'Industria,* No. 2, April-June, pp. 175-201.

23. Although state aid averaged at around 8 per cent of net sales from 1982 to 1990, net losses amounted to L 365 billion in 1990 exceeding net capital estimated at L 281 billion. In 1991, under the increasing burden of interest charges, losses climbed to L 663 billion in spite of L 500 billion of public endowment funds, prompting the government in 1992 to start liquidation. The precarious financial situation of EFIM was worsened in 1990-1991 by several exogenous factors, such as the fall in the prices of aluminium and the fall in defence orders, due to changes in the international environment.

24. Default risk concerns especially loans to Federconsorzi, a bankrupt institution, and to Iraq by the Atlanta branch.

25. In the industrial sector, two kinds of enterprises were considered for sale: those that did not fit in well with the overall portfolio or strategic aims of the public conglomerates; and loss-making enterprises that were draining the financial resources of the conglomerates.

26. The prevalence of financial and strategic motivations over productive efficiency goals implied a substantial indifference to issues relating to competition policy in the course of the privatisation process of the 1980s. Anti-trust legislation was introduced only in 1990.

27. Over the 1983-1987 period, privatisation proceeds were estimated at around L 6 trillion for IRI and L 1.5 trillion for ENI (World Bank, *op. cit.*). Over the 1982-1985 period, one third of the financial requirements of IRI were met by privatisation proceeds (Aronica, A., 1989), "Le privatizzazioni nelle partecipazioni satali: uno studio di casi", in A. Di Majo (ed.), *Le politiche di privatizzazioni in Italia,* il Mulino.

28. In some cases, the sale of loss-making firms required the provision by the state of substantial restructuring funds to the buyer or assumption by the state of most of their debts. Private sales were often preferred to market placements, because these financial arrangements were achieved more easily on a bilateral basis.

29. These equity transactions have led to a sizeable increase in the number of public enterprises quoted in the Italian and foreign stock markets. Over the 1984-1988 period five IRI subsidiaries and four ENI subsidiaries were listed.

30. Alfa Romeo was responsible for about 80 per cent of total losses of IRI in the mechanical engineering sector.

31. The sale of Crediop yielded proceeds for the central government budget, but its so-called privatisation amounted to a mere change in status of the special-credit institution within the state-controlled sector.

32. After a period of financial consolidation and industrial restructuring, an agreement had been reached in the spring of 1985 between IRI and a private group (Buitoni) for the sale of Sme for about L 0.5 trillion. In spite of its initial agreement to the operation, the government stopped the privatisation of Sme after the interventions of the interministerial committee for industrial policy (CIPI) and the parliament.

Annex II

Supporting statistical material to Part III

Table A1. **Efficiency and quality of public services: selected indicators**

A. Efficiency gap[1]		Italy	EC	G7 countries
Rail transport	1981-83	36	54	55
Postal services	1975-84	30	55	67
Air transport	1976-86	88	94	94
B. TFP growth[2]				
Rail transport	1970-83	-0.1	1.3	1.0
Telephone services	1984-88	4.0	3.9	3.8
Air transport	1976-86	2.8	1.3	1.6

C. Quality of services			Italy	Germany	France	United Kingdom	Spain	United States
Postal services	Average delivery delay within 500 km (in days)	1987	3.5	1.0	1.3	1.0	–	2.0
Telephone services	Successful urban calls (%)	1989	50.5	99.0	70.3	86.0[3]	–	–
	Successful intercity calls (%)	1989	52.4	57.9	72.8	–	–	–
	Average delay for telephone connection (in months)	Various years[4]	0.6	1.1	0.6	3.0	3.7	–

1. Actual output relative to optimal output for a given input mix.
2. Average compounded growth rates.
3. 1988.
4. Italy: 1991; Germany: 1989; France: 1987; United Kingdom: 1987; Spain: 1987.

Sources: OECD (1991), *Survey of Italy 1990-1991*; Prosperetti, L. (1992), "I servizi di pubblica utilità", *Previsioni dell'economia italiana*, No. 2, Confindustria; Prosperetti, L. (1992), "Efficienza e qualità nei principali servizi di pubblica utilità: l'Italia nel contesto internazionale", *L'industria*, No. 2, April-June; Rubino, P. (1993), "Costo e qualità nei servizi pubblici: tre casi", *Competere in Europa*, S. Rossi (ed.).

Table A2. Labour productivity in public services

			Italy	Germany	France	United Kingdom	Spain	United States
A. Labour productivity level								
Rail transport	Traffic/employee	1990	100.0	135.6	174.6	112.2	–	–
Telephone services	Subscribers/employee	1988	100.0	70.2	85.2	52.3	–	–
	Conversations/employee	1988	100.0	76.6	90.4	63.2	–	–
Electricity	Subscribers/employee	1988	100.0	–	93.9	74.3	–	–
B. Labour productivity growth[1]								
Rail transport	Traffic/employee	1970-91	2.0	2.6	2.2	–	3.7	5.9
		1985-91	6.5	3.7	2.9	5.5	5.6	8.6
Postal services	Letters/employee	1975-90	0.6	0.8	1.0	-0.3	–	1.1
		1985-90	3.8	1.0	4.5	-3.2	–	0.8
Telephone services	Subscribers/employee	1973-90	4.5	4.2	8.7	–	–	5.6
		1985-90	3.6	3.9	5.7	–	3.7	4.5
	Conversations/employee	1973-90	5.4	4.1	8.0	–	–	–
		1985-90	6.4	2.4	8.3	–	9.6	–
Electricity	Energy/employee	1970-91	4.3	–	5.0	3.5[2]	–	1.0[2]
		1985-91	4.8	2.5[3]	5.7	2.8[3]	–	3.7[3]

			Italy	Atlas group[4]	15 companies[5]
Air transport	Traffic/employee	1970-91	3.2	4.3	4.3
		1985-91	4.4	0.4	0.9

1. Average compounded growth rates.
2. 1970-89.
3. 1985-90.
4. Alitalia, Air France, Iberia, Lufthansa and Sabena.
5. Atlas group plus American Airlines, British Caledonian, British Airways, JAL, KLM, PanAm, Qantas, SAS, Swissair, TWA, Varig.

Sources: OECD (1991), *Survey of Italy 1990-1991*; Prosperetti, L. (1992), "I servizi di pubblica utilità", *Previsioni dell'economia italiana*, No. 2, Confindustria; Prosperetti, L. (1992), "Efficienza e qualità nei principali servizi di pubblica utilità: l'Italia nel contesto internazionale", *L'industria*, No. 2, April-June; Rubino, P. (1993), "Costo e qualità nei servizi pubblici: tre casi", *Competere in Europa*, S. Rossi (ed.).

Table A3. **Financial indicators for the main public enterprises, 1980-1992**[1]

	1980	1983	1986	1989	1991	1992
	Trillions of lire					
Net sales						
IRI	n.a.	41.09	52.58	66.75	79.90	82.99
ENI	23.02	38.30	33.52	37.19	50.88	49.78
EFIM	2.46	3.96	4.18	4.62[6]	4.56	n.a.
ENEL	n.a.	n.a.	n.a.	22.34	26.82	29.19[8]
	Percentage of net sales					
Net profits						
IRI	–	–7.8	–1.1	1.9	–1.2	–5.4
IRI[2]	–	–7.3	0.2	2.5	–0.8	–5.1
ENI	0.3	3.8	1.6	4.2	2.0	1.9
EFIM	–3.6	–19.8	–4.9	–0.6[6]	–14.5	–
ENEL	–	–	–	0.7	0.9	0.8[8]
Net financial charges						
IRI	–	15.2	7.2	5.7	7.5	9.6
ENI	2.9	4.9	3.6	4.1	4.3	4.9
EFIM	9.2	14.7	9.8	11.5[6]	–	–
ENEL	–	–	–	11.3	13.4	11.7[8]
State aid[3]						
IRI	–	9.8	6.1	1.3	0.6	0.1
ENI	1.5	4.6	0.3	0.3	–	–
EFIM	4.1	15.0	15.9	0.3	11.0[7]	–
ENEL	–	–	–	–	–	–
Net debt						
IRI	–	87.9	65.4	68.4	79.3	87.4
ENI	39.3	45.4	43.3	42.9	45.8	57.1
EFIM	64.1	76.2	82.4	99.9[6]	185.3	–
ENEL	–	–	–	123.0	117.9	108.4[9]
Capital						
IRI[4]	–	35.4	44.5	32.9	27.8	22.8
ENI[5]	10.8	14.1	27.6	35.3	32.0	32.6
EFIM	–	8.4	19.1	16.0[6]	6.2[7]	–
ENEL	–	–	–	67.7	59.7	56.8[9]

1. Data for IRI refer to industrial activities.
2. Including banks.
3. Includes BEI loans and bond issues with principal and interest guaranteed by state.
4. Excludes GEPI.
5. Includes net profits.
6. 1988.
7. 1990.
8. Provisional.
9. First semester.

Sources: Ministero delle Partecipazioni Statali; Ministry of Industry; The Treasury (1992), *Libro verde sulle partecipazioni dello stato e Allegati*; CIRIEC (1992), *Le riforme mancate*, Franco Angeli, Milano.

Table A4.   **IRI and ENI: Financial indicators of main non-financial subsidiaries, 1991**

Company	Type of activity	Profitability [1]	Leverage [2]	Financial charges [3]
		IRI		
Sme	Manufacturing	+++	–0.1	–0.5
Stet [4]	Telecommunications/Public service	+++	1.0	5.7
Rai	Telecommunications/Public service	+++	4.5	3.9
Finmeccanica	Manufacturing	—++	2.1	2.7
Alitalia	Transportation	—++	0.8	1.9
Iritecna	Plant engineering	—++ ——+ [5]	1.9	9.5
Finmare	Transportation	—+	4.5	5.1
Ilva	Iron and steel	—+	2.1	7.8
Fincantieri	Shipbuilding	—— [6]	1.1	1.7
		ENI		
Agip	Energy	+++	0.5 [7]	1.3 [7]
Agip Petroli	Energy	+++		
Snam	Energy/Public service	+++	1.5	4.2
Nuovo Pignone	Manufacturing	+++	0.9	2.6
Snam Progetti	Plant engineering	+++	–1.6	–2.3
Saipem	Plant engineering	—+	0.4	2.9
Enichem [8]	Manufacturing	—+	0.7	n.a.
Enirisorse	Mining/Metallurgy	——	1.2	3.9
Enichem agricoltura	Manufacturing	——	1.3	n.a.
Savio	Manufacturing	——	5.5	3.5
Sogedit	Publishing	——	0.4	1.0

1. +++ = Positive net operating result (includes financial charges and depreciation).
   —++ = Positive operating result (excludes financial charges).
   —+ = Positive gross operating margin (excludes financial charges and depreciation).
   —— = Negative gross operation margin.
2. Ratio of debt to capital.
3. Percentage of net sales.
4. Including Finsiel.
5. Excluding highway operation.
6. Excluding state subsidies.
7. Agip and Agip Petroli consolidated.
8. Excluding Enichem Agricoltura.
Sources: The Treasury (1992), *Libro verde sulle partecipazioni dello stato.*

Table A5. **Financial indicators of main public banks, 1991**

	Ordinary credit						Special credit
	Comit[1]	Credit[1]	S. Paolo	Monte Paschi	Cariplo	BNL	IMI
	Trillions of lire						
Net profits	0.32	0.29	0.44	0.24	0.23	0.07	0.23
Interest margin[2]	2.43	2.0	1.82	1.65	2.16	2.54	0.53
Intermediation margin[3]	3.5	2.85	2.58	2.33	2.93	3.68	0.63
Financial proceeds	9.62	8.14	8.64	5.49	6.46	10.24	3.33
Total net assets	102.60	89.37	n.a.	n.a.	n.a.	99.17	40.19
	Percentage of proceeds						
Net profits	3.33	3.56	5.06	4.33	3.58	0.72	6.90
Interest margin	25.26	24.57	21.03	30.06	33.44	24.76	15.79
Intermediation margin	36.38	35.01	29.92	42.42	45.29	35.89	18.79
Memorandum item:							
Capital/asset ratio (%)	4.6	4.40	4.80	5.70	6.00	4.90	10.40
Interest margin/intermediation margin (%)	69	70	71	71	74	69	84

1. Not consolidated data.
2. Difference between interest received and interest paid.
3. Interest margin plus other intermediation proceeds (*e.g.* capital and foreign exchange gains, dividends).
Source: The Treasury (1992), *Libro verde sulle partecipazioni dello stato* and *Allegati*.

Table A6. **Credits of public banks to public enterprises, 1989-1992**[1]

	1989			1992		
	Billions of lire	Percentage of total credit to public entities	Percentage of credit to public entities by public banks	Billions of lire	Percentage of total credit to public entities	Percentage of credit to public entities by public banks
Borrower						
Public conglomerates	39 771	81.9	70.8	53 076	85.8	64.1
Autonomous agencies	10 861	99.1	19.3	17 444	97.9	21.1
Other public enterprises	5 810	87.7	10.3	12 298	88.1	14.8
TOTAL	56 442	85.0	100.0	82 818	88.5	100.0
Per cent of total financial investment	13.0			12.1		

1. Public banks include *Istituti di Credito di Diritto Pubblico, Banche d'interesse nazionale, Casse di risparmio* and Istituti di credito speciale.
Source: Bank of Italy.

Table A7. **IRI group privatisations, 1983-1992**

Billions of lire

	1983	1984	1985	1986	1987	1988	1989	1990	1991	1992	Total
A. Total sales											
Banking	144	176	290	21	123	147	129	241	0	0	1 271
Industry/ manufacturing	88	13	61	169	1 030	8	267	43	0	425	2 104
Total	232	189	351	190	1 153	155	396	284	0	425	3 375
B. Partial sales											
New issues	0	0	374	299	0	0	0	0	104	0	777
Sale of shares	131	106	1 771	211	25	1 085	1 664	502	879	1 642	8 016
Sale of warrants	58	69	112	382	229	395	303	132	27	0	1 707
Total	189	175	2 257	892	254	1 480	1 967	634	1 010	1 642	10 500
C. Total divestiture (A + B)	421	364	2 608	1 082	1 407	1 635	2 363	918	1 010	2 067	13 875

Source: IRI.

Table A8. **Weight of public enterprises in total employment of non-agricultural business sector by main branches of activity, 1988**

	Energy and mining	Industry	Transport and communication	Finance and insurance	Distribution	Total
West Germany	60.0	1.1	70.0	30.6	2.0	8.8
France	78.5	12.7	59.0	34.0	2.8	13.3
Italy	**85.4**	**10.1**	**81.4**	**50.0**	**1.0**	**15.8**
United Kingdom	67.0	1.0	32.0	n.a.	n.a.	6.0
Belgium	23.7	0.1	63.5	8.4	0.1	9.8
Netherlands	2.0	2.2	43.7	2.0	n.a.	6.0
Luxembourg	n.a.	n.a.	31.9	10.6	n.a.	4.7
Denmark	88.0	0.5	57.6	1.0	n.a.	8.5
Ireland	71.3	1.4	79.7	32.0	1.8	10.7
Greece	62.0	1.3	45.0	31.0	3.0	15.0
Spain	41.0	3.7	32.0	3.0	0.2	7.5
Portugal	57.3	6.6	68.7	95.0	2.0	14.5

Source: CEEP (1990), *L'entreprise publique dans la Communauté Économique Européenne: Annales CEEP*, Brussels.

135

Table A9. **State holdings in industry and services in the major 1 898 enterprises, 1991**[1]

	Share of public employment in total (%)	Share of public enterprises in total (%)	Number of public enterprises with rank ≤10	Number of public enterprises with rank ≤20	Number of public enterprises with rank ≤50
Food and agriculture	8.10	3.37	0	0	0
Electronics	22.50	24.42	0	0	1
Plant engineering and installation	52.28	33.96	0	0	0
Mechanical	20.53	9.52	0	0	1
Iron and steel	49.28	23.88	1	1	1
Chemicals	30.90	8.96	0	1	2
Vehicles	23.83	15.71	0	1	2
Energy	52.34	26.92	2	3	4
Public services	93.69	70.73	2	2	3
Mining	93.28	54.55	1	1	1
Transportation	73.58	27.50	0	1	1
Advertising, film	72.58	31.25	0	1	1
Retailing	23.11	20.83	0	0	1
Domestic appliances	3.22	6.82	0	0	0
Rubber	7.95	7.14	0	0	0
Clothing	0.00	0.00	0	0	0
Trading, import/export	0.00	0.00	0	0	0
Textile	0.00	0.00	0	0	0
Pharmaceuticals	0.00	0.00	0	0	0
Synthetic fibers	41.33	43.75	0	0	0
Building products	3.00	6.78	0	0	0
Beverages	0.00	0.00	0	0	0
Civil engineering and building	9.62	18.00	0	0	0
Paper	7.89	9.09	0	0	0
Glass	20.51	19.23	0	0	0
Publishing	9.17	14.29	0	0	0
Leather goods	0.00	0.00	0	0	0
Other manufacturing	8.87	7.14	0	0	0
TOTAL	28.52	12.49	60	55	36

1. Enterprises ranked according to net sales.
Source: Mediobanca (1992), *Le principali società italiana*, Milano.

Table A10. **Presence of the State in finance and insurance, 1991**

	Holding	Share[1]	Employees	Financial investment[2]	Deposits[2]	Counters
A. Finance						
Banks of national interest						
Comit	IRI	54.4	18 838	9.8	8.0	581
Credit	IRI	58.1	16 242	8.4	7.1	484
Public law credit institutions						
BNL	Treasury	57.5	21 459	9.3	8.1	489
Banco di Napoli			12 076	5.9	5.5	649
S. Paolo di Torino			13 173	8.6	8.0	456
Monte dei Paschi di Siena			11 820	5.2	5.3	621
Banco di Sicilia			8 796	4.5	3.7	344
Banco di Sardegna			2 603	0.8	0.9	88
Ordinary credit banks						
Banca Creditwest	IRI	68	415	0.1	0.1	20
Banca di Legnano	IRI	55.3	736	0.3	0.2	50
Banco di Chiavari	IRI	71	837	0.2	0.3	57
Banca Sicula	IRI	51	576	0.1	0.1	61
Banca Fideuram	IMI	81	707	0.3	0.2	12
Savings banks			80 483	22.0	23.0	n.a.
Special credit institutions						
Fonspa	IRI		437	0.1	0.7	1
Credito immobiliare	BNL	100	n.a.			
Credito mobiliare	BNL	100	n.a.			
Credito cin. e teatrale	BNL	100	n.a.			
Efibanca	BNL	52	424	1.6	1.1	6
IMI	Treasury	50	967	4.7	3.0	11
Crediop	S. Paolo di Torino Cassa Depositi e Prestiti	100	402	4.8	3.3	8
Total			190 366			4 005
Percentage share[3]			58.4	86.7	78.6	

	Holding	Share[1]	Premia[4]	Rank[5]
B. Insurance				
INA	INA	100	7.1	3
Assitalia	INA	60	5.1	5
Fideuram vita	IMI	100	1.2	14
Padana Assicurazioni	ENI	100	0.5	38
Sasa	IRI	99.8	0.2	80
Percentage share			14.1	

1. Ownership share of public holding calculated on total capital (ordinary and saving shares).
2. Percentage share over total.
3. Over total employment, financial investment and deposits.
4. Share over total premia.
5. Rank by premia among all insurance companies.

Sources: IRI; Bank of Italy (1991), *Relazione Annuale*, Appendice, Tables aD9, aD10 and aD16; *Sole-24 Ore*, 17 July 1992; Mediobanca (1992), *Le principali società italiana*, Milano; The Treasury (1992), *Libro verde sulle partecipazioni dello stato*.

Table A11. **State-owned enterprises in the business sector**

A. Public conglomerates and public utilities

	Activity	Status	Shareholder[3]	Employees[4]
Conglomerates				
IRI		Public holding	Treasury	335 600
ENI		Public holding	Treasury	124 032
EFIM		Public agency[1]		37 100
GEPI		Public holding	IRI, ENI, EFIM, IMI	31 100
Public utilities				
Poste	Mail service	Autonomous agency[2]		237 000
FS	Railways	Public holding	Treasury, Ministries of Budget and Transportation	207 000
ENEL	Electricity	Public holding	Treasury	107 431
Other				
Monopoli	Tobacco, salt	Public holding	Treasury, Ministries of Budget and Finance	14 496
ANAS	Road maintenance	Autonomous agency		12 470

B. Credit institutions

	Activity	Status	Shareholder[3]	Employees[4]
Banks of national interest				
Credit	Commercial banking	Public holding	IRI	34 455
Comit	Commercial banking	Public holding	IRI	
Public-law credit institutions				
BNL	Universal banking	Public holding	Treasury	69 927
Banco di Napoli	Commercial banking	Public holding		
S. Paolo di Torino	Commercial banking	Public holding		
Banco di Sicilia	Commercial banking	Public holding		
Monte Paschi Siena	Commercial banking	Public agency		
Banco di Sardegna	Commercial banking	Public holding		
Savings banks				
Various	Commercial banking	Foundations and public agencies		80 483

Ordinary credit banks

Banca Creditwest	Commercial banking	Public holding	IRI	
Banca di Legnano	Commercial banking	Public holding	IRI	
Banco di Chiavari	Commercial banking	Public holding	IRI	
Banca Sicula	Commercial banking	Public holding	IRI	
Banca Fideuram	Commercial banking	Public holding	IMI	3 271

Special credit institutions

Fonspa	Special credit	Public holding	IRI	
IMI	Special credit	Public holding	Treasury	
Crediop	Special credit	Public holding	San Paolo di Torino, Cassa Depositi e Prestiti	
Subsidiaries of BNL	Special credit	Public holding	BNL	2 230

C. Other public financial institutions

	Status	Shareholder[3]
Insurance		
Ina	Public holding	Treasury
Assitalia	Public holding	INA
Fideuram Vita	Public holding	IMI
Padana Assicuraz.	Public holding	ENI
Sasa	Public holding	IRI
Financial services		
Cofiri	Public holding	IRI
Sofid	Public holding	IRI
ENI Intl. Hold.	Public holding	ENI
Serfi	Public holding	ENI
Sige	Public holding	IMI
Leasing and factoring		
Ifitalia	Public holding	BNL
Locafit	Public holding	BNL

1. Liquidation procedures started in July 1992.
2. To be transformed into a public agency in 1994.
3. Ministry or financial holding.
4. Sources: Ministry of Industry for IRI, ENI, EFIM, GEPI and Enel; ISTAT (1992), *Statistiche sulla amministrazione pubblica* for Monopoli, ANAS, FS and Poste; Mediobanca (1992), *Le principali società italiana*; and Bank of Italy (1992), *Relazione Annuale*, Appendice, Table aD16, for credit institutions.

Source: OECD.

Table A12. **Structure and sectoral ramification of public conglomerates (non-financial)**

Sectoral holdings	Share (%)	Employees	Number of subsidiaries	Main sectors of activity
IRI s.p.a. (1992)				
Finmeccanica	94.4	51 450	85	Aeronautics; space; defence; civil engineering; energy; transports; manufacturing; automation; biomedics; electronics
Stet	52.2	137 900	104	Telecommunication services and industry; plant engineering; electronics; publishing; data processing and communication; research
Sme	62.1	20 450	52	Food and allied products; retailing; catering
Ilva	99.99	41 300	143	Iron and steel; metallurgy; mining
Iritecna	100.0	24 650	91	Building and civil engineering; plant engineering and installation; urban infrastructure
Fincantieri	99.99	16 150	4	Shipbuilding
Finmare	99.98	7 350	18	Sea transportation
Alitalia	86.4	28 900	21	Air transportation; airport operation
Rai	99.6	15 950	10	Television; advertising; film; publishing
ENI s.p.a. (1991)				
Agip	100.0	9 422	34	Oil and gas exploration, production and sale; renewable energy sources
AgipPetroli	100.0	23 987	50	Supply, refinement and distribution of oil; energy-saving services
Snam	99.99	18 523	60	Supply, transportation, distribution and sale of gas
Snamprogetti	100.0	45 030	12	Plant engineering and installation (chemical, petrochemical, ecologic, infrastructure)
Saipem	78.6	9 863	13	Drilling; plant engineering and installation; civil infrastructure
Enichem	99.4	37 264	106	Basic chemicals and chemical products (fibres, fertilisers, plastic, etc.)
Enirisorse	100.0	8 299	27	Mining, production, transformation and sale of non-ferrous metals; coal mining; chemicals
Nuovo Pignone	71.3	5 344	6	Machinery and equipment for oil and gas, chemical, electric, nuclear and textile industries
Savio	99.99	1 988	3	Machinery and equipment for textile industry
Sogedit	100.0	765	3	Publishing

EFIM[1] (1991)

Alumix	7 275		Metallurgy; manufacturing of iron, steel and non-ferrous products
Aviofer Breda	20 000		Manufacturing of vehicles; aerospace
Fin. Ernesto Breda			Metallurgy; defence systems
Efim impianti	2 031		Mechanical, electrical engineering and allied trades
Siv	5 220		Glass and glass containers
GEPI s.p.a (1991)	Owned by IMI, IRI, ENI and EFIM	31 000	133	Ordinary activity is aimed at relieving temporary sectoral crises (through acquisition of shares, creation of new firms or provision of funds). Extraordinary activity is aimed at relocating excess manpower (through creation of new firms and implementation of labour mobility schemes).

1. Public management agency, *Ente di gestione*, under liquidation.

Sources: IRI; Ministry of Industry: The Treasury (1992), *Libro verde sulle partecipazioni dello stato*; Gruppo IRI (1992), *Annuario 1991-1992*; ENI (1992), *Bilancio Consolidato 1991*; *Sole 24-Ore*, 17 July 1992; Aronica, A. (1992), "Problemi di economicità ed equità nel ritorno al mercato dei gruppi pubblici. La questione EFIM", *Tentativo di descrizione di un agenda di governo*, OIKOS, Roma.

Table A13. **Public services**

	Electricity			Gas					Telecommunications		
							Distribution		Telephone[5]		Television
	Imports	Production	Distribution	Imports	Production	Transportation	Snam[3]	Local	Stet[6]	Iritel[7]	Rai
Company	Enel	Enel	Enel	Snam	Agip	Snam	Snam	Local	Stet[6]	Iritel[7]	Rai
Market share	100	84	93	100	90	96	26	46	100	100	49
Type	PH	PH	PH	PSH	PSH	PSH	PSH	PA	PSH	PSH	PSH
Owner	Treasury	Treasury	Treasury	ENI	ENI	ENI	ENI	..	IRI	IRI	IRI
Regime	SC	SC[1]	SC[2]	M	M	M[4]	M	LC	SC	SC	SC
Concession/monitoring regulation	Ministry of Industry, CIPE			Ministry of Industry, CIPE				Local authorities	PT Ministry		PT Ministry, Authority for information,[8] Parliament
Tariffs	CIP	CIP	CIP	CIP	CIP	CIP	CIP		PT Ministry, Budget, Treasury		PT Ministry

PH   Public holding
PSH   Public sub-holding or subsidiary
PA   Public agency (includes special and autonomous agencies)
SC   State concession
LC   Local concession
M   Monopoly
CIPE *Comitato Interministeriale per la Programmazione Economica*
LM   Legal monopoly
CIPET *Comitato Interministeriale per la Politica dei Trasporti*
CIP   *Comitato Interministeriale Prezzi*

1. Production has been partially liberalised in 1991.
2. Includes also exports and sales.
3. Mainly through the subsidiary Italgas.
4. Transportation has been partially liberalised in 1991.
5. Terminals and value-added services liberalised according to EC *Green Book* (1987) and *Open Network Provision* (1990).
6. City and continental network ensured by the subsidiary Sip, inter-continental by Italcable and satellite by Telespazio.
7. Intercity network. Formerly *Azienda di Stato per i Servizi Telefonici*.
8. *Autorità garante per le radiodiffusioni e l'editoria*.

Table A13. **Public services** *(cont.)*

| | Transportation | | | | | | Mail | Water cycle | Waste disposal |
| | Rail | Air | Domestic sea cabotage | Highways | Local transport | | | | |
					Subway	Bus			
Company	Ferrovie dello Stato	Alitalia/Ati Aeroporti Roma	Tirrenia Others	Società autostrade	Local	Local	Poste	Local	Local
Type	PH	PSH	PSH	PSH	PA, PSH	PA, PH	PA	PA	PA, PH
Owner	Ministries of Budget, Treasury & Transportation	IRI	IRI	IRI	..	..	..	..	..
Market share	100	86	n.a.	100	100	n.a.	100	96	63[14]
Regime	SC[9]	SC[10]	SC[11]	SC[10]	LM, LC[12]	LM, LC	LM[13]	LM	LM, LC
Concession/ monitoring/ regulation	Min. of Transportation CIPET	Min. of Transportation	Min. Marina	ANAS	Local authorities	Local authorities	PT Ministry	Local authorities	Local authorities
Tariffs	Ministry of Transportation	..	..	Min. of Public Works	Local authorities	Local authorities	PT Ministry, Budget, Treasury		

PH   Public holding
PSH   Public sub-holding or subsidiary
PA   Public agency (includes special and autonomous agencies)
SC   State concession
LC   Local concession
M   Monopoly
CIPE *Comitato Interministeriale per la Programmazione Economica*
LM   Legal monopoly
CIPET *Comitato Interministeriale per la Politica del Trasporti*
CIP   *Comitato Interministeriale Prezzi*

9. A few state concessions to private companies also exist.
10. Non-exclusive state concession.
11. Exclusive concession only for some services (e.g. mail).
12. Concessions granted only to public agencies or public holdings.
13. Concessions to private companies are allowed for some services (e.g. express mail).
14. In cities with more than 20 000 inhabitants (1984).

Sources: The Treasury (1992), *Libro verde sulle partecipazioni dello stato e Allegati*; Alta autorità per l'esercizio della concorrenza; Rubino, P. (1993), "Costo e qualità dei servizi pubblici: tre casi", *Competere in Europa*, S. Rossi (ed.); Ciò, A. (1992), "Regolamentazione e concorrenza nei servizi di pubblica utilità: il caso del gas", *L'industria*, il Mulino, No. 2, April-June; Fraquelli G. (1992), "Regolamentazione e concorrenza nei servizi du pubblica utilità: il caso dell'energia elettrica", *L'industria*, il Mulino, No. 2, April-June; Fornengo, G. (1992), "Regolamentazione e concorrenza nei servizi di pubblica utilità: il caso dell'acqua", *L'industria*, il Mulino, No. 2, April-June; Pontarollo, E. and A. Costa (1992), "Regolamentazione e concorrenza nei servizi di pubblica utilità: il caso delle telecomunicazioni", *L'industria*, il Mulino, No. 2, April-June; Ferrara, G. (1992), "Regolamentazione e concorrenza nei servizi di trasporto: il caso del trasporto marittimo", *L'industria*, il Mulino, No. 2, April-June; CIRIEC.

Table A14. **Main public enterprises listed in Italian and foreign stock markets, 1993**

Percentage shares in brackets

Companies	Market capitalisation on Milan Stock Exchange (Lira billion)[6]	Estimated shareholders[7]	Presence in foreign stock exchanges
Candidates for privatisation			
Banca Commerciale Italiana (IRI)	5 499.3	34 000	Yes
Credito Italiano (IRI)	4 377.1	38 500	Yes
Sme (IRI)	2 956.0	20 000	
Nuovo Pignone (ENI)	792.7	2 000	
Sip (IRI)	10 471.8	63 000	Yes
Stet (IRI)	10 035.7	28 000	Yes
Italcable (IRI)	1 695.0	7 200	
Assitalia (INA)	1 392.8	47 800	
Banca Fideuram (IMI)	911.4	38 000	
Breda Finanziaria (EFIM)[4]	119.9	5 400	
TOTAL	38 251.7	283 900	
	(18.5)		
Other			
Enichem (ENI)	4 058.8	3 000	
Sirti (IRI)	2 053.7	10 000	
Italgas (ENI)	1 942.5	27 000	Yes
Saipem (ENI)	1 298.1	1 700	
Alitalia (IRI)	823.7	20 000	
Immobiliare Metanopoli (ENI)	584.3	3 150	
Autostrade (IRI)[1]	570.8	25 000	
Credito Fondiario (IRI)	530.9	2 600	
Finmeccanica (IRI)[2]	524.2	5 600	
Dalmine (IRI)	453.4	8 500	
BNL (Tesoro)[3]	422.8	75 000	
Ansaldo Trasporti (IRI)	270.4	3 000	
Banca di Legnano (IRI)	270.2	4 400	
Montefibre (ENI)	259.8	6 100	
Banco di Chiavari (IRI)	247.1	7 500	
Enichem Augusta (ENI)	204.0	2 000	
Serfi (ENI)	151.2	3 300	
Condotte Acque Torino (ENI)	102.2	600	
Fiar (IRI)	83.7	1 700	
Garboli (IRI)[5]	7.0	220	
TOTAL	14 858.4	230 600	
	(7.2)		
GRAND TOTAL	53 110.1		
	(25.6)		
Memorandum items:			
Total IRI	40 870	299 400	
	(19.7)		
Total ENI	9 393.2	48 900	
	(4.5)		
Total other	2 846.9	166 200	
	(1.4)		
Total market capitalisation	207 165		

1. Preferred stocks only.
2. Estimates.
3. Saving shares only.
4. Suspended at the end of 1992.
5. Roma Stock Exchange.
6. May 1993.
7. October 1993.
Source: Consob Economic Research Dept.

Annex III

Chronology of main economic events

Fiscal policy

1992

September

Presentation of the state budget for 1993 aimed at cutting L 93 trillion from a trend deficit estimated at L 243 trillion, with additional revenues accounting for L 49.5 trillion of the proposed reduction in the deficit. This would leave the deficit at L 150 trillion. On the expenditure side, savings worth L 43.5 trillion are expected to result from structural reform measures in the domain of health services, pension payments, local authority finance and the public labour market.

October

Through a Delegation Law the Amato Government obtains from Parliament special powers to cut primary spending in four main areas (health services, pension payments, local authority finance and public labour market).

1993

April

Following referendum results, formation of new Government under Mr. Ciampi, the former Governor of the Bank of Italy.

May

In the face of renewed deficit slippage, the Government announces a package of fiscal restraint worth L 12.4 trillion or 0.8 per cent of GDP to hold the state deficit to a relaxed target of L 155 trillion. The fiscal package is almost equally split between expenditure cuts and revenue gains.

July

Presentation of the Government's medium-term fiscal programme, aimed at stabilising the public debt as a percentage of GDP by 1995 and reducing the state budget deficit to 6.8 per cent of GDP in 1996.

August

Adoption of new electoral law.

The Government announces accelerated spending (L 10 trillion) on public works, especially transport infrastructure and new buildings.

September

Presentation of the state budget for 1994 aimed at cutting the deficit to L 144 trillion or 8.7 per cent of GDP. For the first time in many years, the budget proposals rely almost entirely on expenditure cuts.

Monetary policy and financial markets

1992

September

Increase in discount rate to 15 per cent and increase in the rate on fixed-term advances to 16.5 per cent.

Increase in penalty rate applied to banks failing to comply with the compulsory reserve requirements from 5 to 10 percentage points.

Realignment of EMS currencies reducing the central value of the lira by 7 per cent.

Suspension of the lira from the European Exchange Rate Mechanism.

Creation of Italian Futures Market (MIF).

October

Introduction of foreign currency swaps.

The Bank of Italy calls on the credit institutions to keep the rise in lira lending within confines set out in a six-month monitoring programme.

Cut in discount rate to 14 per cent and in the rate on fixed-term advances to 16 per cent.

November

Cut in discount rate to 13 per cent and in the rate on fixed-term advances to 15 per cent.

December

Cut in discount rate to 12 per cent and in the rate on fixed-term advances to 13 per cent.

1993

February

Cut in discount rate to 11.5 per cent and in the rate on fixed-term advances to 12.5 per cent.

Reduction in compulsory reserve requirements from 22.5 per cent to 17.5 per cent.

March

Reduction in reserve ratio to 10 per cent for certificates of deposits (CDs) with maturities of eighteen months or more.

April

Cut in discount rate to 11 per cent.

Adoption of law on the creation of private pension funds.

May

Cut in discount rate to 10.5 per cent and in the rate on fixed-term advances to 11.5 per cent.

June

Cut in discount rate to 10 per cent and in the rate on fixed-term advances to 11 per cent.

July

Cut in discount rate to 9 per cent and in the rate on fixed-term advances to 10 per cent. The interest paid on compulsory reserves against CDs is lowered from 8.5 per cent to 6.5 per cent.

August

Adoption of new banking law, allowing banks to own shares of non-financial firms (apart from insurance companies). The law embodies the EC second directive on bank co-ordination.

September

Cut in discount rate to 8.5 per cent and in the rate on fixed-term advances to 9.5 per cent. The target range for M2 growth is set at 5 to 7 per cent, unchanged from 1992 and 1993.

October

Cut in discount rate to 8 per cent and in the rate on fixed-term advances to 9 per cent.

Incomes policy

1993

July

New national labour agreement establishing two levels for wage bargaining in the private sector. The Accord also provides for flexible forms of employment contracts.

Privatisation

1992

January

Law 35 provides the legal basis for turning management agencies (enti di gestione), public agencies (enti pubblici) and autonomous companies (aziende autonome) into joint-stock corporations.

Public railways (Ferrovie dello Stato), formerly an autonomous company, are turned into a joint-stock corporation.

July

Decree 487 starts procedures for the liquidation of EFIM, the third largest public conglomerate employing 37 000 people. Reimbursement of EFIM's debt by the state spurs a dispute over state aid with the EC Commission.

August

Law 359 streamlines procedures for privatisation by turning a number of state-owned enterprises into joint-stock corporations and centralising in the Treasury authority over decisions concerning their management.

Reduction in the size and changes in the composition of the board of directors of the main public enterprises.

November

The Treasury presents to the Government the "Reorganisation plan of IRI, ENI, ENEL, INA, BNL and IMI" contemplating the full privatisation important public companies, utilities and financial institutions.

December

The reorganisation plan is approved by Parliament and Government.

A resolution of CIPE identifies companies to be privatised first – Credito Italiano (IRI), INA, Nuovo Pignone (ENI) and the industrial activities of Sme (IRI) – and makes sale procedures more transparent.

1993

April

First report of the Government on the state of privatisations.

Resolution of CIPE setting the general criteria for the reorganisation of telecommunication services in view of their privatisation.

Suppression of the Ministry of State Participations (Ministero delle Partecipazioni Statali) by national referendum.

June

Creation of a permanent Committee for privatisations (Comitato di consulenza globale e di garanzia) advising the Treasury on the implementation of the privatisation plan.

July

Sale of Siv (EFIM).

Sale of Italgel (Sme).

Agreement with the EC Commission on the reimbursement of EFIM's debt.

August

Procedures started for selling IMI by public offer.

Reorganisation of telecommunication services approved by Government.

September

Sale of Cirio-Bertolli-De Rica (Sme).

Procedures started for selling Banca Commerciale Italiana and Credito Italiano by public offer.

Government decree paving the way for public offer sales and defining "special powers" to be retained in so-called "strategic" sectors.

Transformation of postal services into a public agency.

December

Sale of Credito Italiano.

STATISTICAL AND STRUCTURAL ANNEX

Selected background statistics

	Average 1983-92	1983	1984	1985	1986	1987	1988	1989	1990	1991	1992
A. Percentage changes											
Private consumption[1]	2.8	0.7	2.0	3.0	3.7	4.2	4.2	3.5	2.5	2.3	1.8
Gross fixed capital formation[1]	2.5	-0.6	3.6	0.6	2.2	5.0	6.9	4.3	3.8	0.6	-1.4
Public investment[1]	7.0	12.5	9.4	9.1	3.9	4.3	7.2	5.6	9.5	7.7	1.0
Private investment[1]	1.5	-2.7	2.5	-1.0	1.8	5.2	6.9	4.0	2.5	-1.1	-2.1
Residential[1]	0.6	4.4	-0.5	-2.8	-2.1	-2.4	1.3	2.4	2.8	3.1	0.6
Non-residential[1]	2.0	-6.6	4.3	0	4.0	9.1	9.5	4.7	2.3	-2.9	-3.3
GDP[1]	2.4	1.0	2.7	2.6	2.9	3.1	4.1	2.9	2.1	1.3	0.9
GDP price deflator	8.2	15.0	11.6	8.8	7.9	6.0	6.6	6.2	7.6	7.4	4.7
Industrial production	1.5	-3.2	3.3	1.2	3.5	3.9	6.0	3.1	0	-1.9	-0.6
Employment	0.5	0.2	0.4	0.4	0.5	-0.2	1.1	0.1	1.8	0.9	-0.6
Compensation of employees (current prices)	10.1	15.1	11.6	11.7	8.0	8.6	10.0	9.5	12.3	9.2	5.1
Productivity (real GDP/employment)	1.9	0.7	2.3	2.2	2.4	3.3	2.9	2.9	0.3	0.4	1.6
Unit labour costs (compensation/real GDP)	7.5	14.0	8.7	8.8	5.0	5.3	5.7	6.4	9.9	7.8	4.2
B. Percentage ratios											
Gross fixed capital formation as per cent of GDP at constant prices	21.3	20.9	21.1	20.7	20.5	20.9	21.5	21.8	22.1	22.0	21.5
Stockbuilding as per cent of GDP at constant prices	1.3	0.5	1.6	1.8	1.7	1.6	1.5	1.1	1.1	1.2	1.2
Foreign balance as per cent of GDP at constant prices	-2.8	-0.9	-1.7	-1.9	-2.0	-3.0	-3.3	-3.2	-3.7	-4.3	-4.4
Compensation of employees as per cent of GDP at current prices	45.4	47.4	46.2	46.2	44.9	44.6	44.2	44.3	45.2	45.4	45.2
Direct taxes as per cent of household income	10.4	9.7	10.1	10.3	10.0	10.0	10.8	10.7	10.7	10.8	10.7
Household saving as per cent of disposable income	17.4	20.2	18.6	17.0	16.7	16.4	15.7	15.8	17.7	17.9	18.2
Unemployment rate	11.2	10.0	10.1	10.2	11.2	12.1	12.1	12.1	11.5	11.0	11.6
C. Other indicator											
Current balance (billion dollars)	-8.3	1.7	-2.3	-3.6	2.4	-1.6	-5.9	-11.0	-14.8	-21.4	-26.6

1. At constant 1985 prices.

Table A. Expenditure on gross domestic product, current prices

Trillions of lire

	1983	1984	1985	1986	1987	1988	1989	1990	1991	1992
Private consumption	396.1	452.4	507.7	559.5	613.9	676.1	744.5	810.4	885.9	951.0
Public consumption	105.1	120.0	135.5	148.3	166.3	186.9	201.4	231.6	253.4	266.9
Gross fixed investment	134.9	152.6	167.6	177.6	194.1	219.2	241.0	266.0	281.7	288.2
Final domestic demand	636.1	725.0	810.7	885.5	974.3	1 082.2	1 186.8	1 307.9	1 421.0	1 506.2
	(15.0)	(14.0)	(11.8)	(9.2)	(10.0)	(11.1)	(9.7)	(10.2)	(8.6)	(6.0)
Stockbuilding	3.3	13.8	15.0	10.9	12.4	15.4	13.7	9.4	10.4	4.3
	(-0.6)	(1.7)	(0.2)	(-0.5)	(0.2)	(0.3)	(-0.1)	(-0.4)	(0.1)	(-0.4)
Total domestic demand	639.4	738.8	825.8	896.4	986.7	1 097.6	1 200.6	1 317.3	1 431.4	1 510.5
	(14.3)	(15.6)	(11.8)	(8.6)	(10.1)	(11.2)	(9.4)	(9.7)	(8.7)	(5.5)
Exports	126.8	150.6	169.0	167.2	176.4	193.7	226.6	249.2	256.2	273.3
Imports	132.9	163.8	184.3	163.8	179.4	199.6	233.9	254.5	261.1	276.6
Foreign balance	-6.0	-13.1	-15.3	3.4	-3.0	-5.9	-7.3	-5.4	-4.9	-3.3
	(1.5)	(-1.1)	(-0.3)	(2.3)	(-0.7)	(-0.3)	(-0.1)	(0.2)	(0.0)	(0.1)
GDP (market prices)	633.3	725.7	810.4	899.8	983.7	1 091.7	1 193.3	1 312.0	1 426.5	1 507.2
	(16.2)	(14.6)	(11.7)	(11.0)	(9.3)	(11.0)	(9.3)	(9.9)	(8.7)	(5.7)

Note: Figures in parentheses are annual growth rates; for stockbuilding and the foreign balance they are contributions to GDP growth.
Source: ISTAT.

155

Table B. **Expenditure on gross domestic product, constant 1985 prices**

Trillions of lire

	1983	1984	1985	1986	1987	1988	1989	1990	1991	1992
Private consumption	483.6	493.2	507.8	526.6	548.6	571.5	591.7	606.3	620.4	631.6
Public consumption	128.2	131.1	135.5	139.0	143.8	147.8	149.1	150.9	153.1	154.7
Gross fixed investment	160.7	166.5	167.6	171.3	179.9	192.4	200.7	208.2	209.6	206.6
Final domestic demand	772.5	790.8	810.9	836.9	872.2	911.6	941.4	965.4	983.1	992.9
	(0.9)	(2.4)	(2.5)	(3.2)	(4.2)	(4.5)	(3.3)	(2.6)	(1.8)	(1.0)
Stockbuilding	3.9	12.9	15.0	13.8	13.9	13.6	10.1	10.3	11.5	11.5
	(−0.6)	(1.2)	(0.3)	(−0.1)	(0.0)	(0.0)	(−0.4)	(0.0)	(0.1)	(0.0)
Total domestic demand	776.4	803.7	825.9	850.7	886.1	925.2	951.5	975.8	994.5	1 004.4
	(0.2)	(3.5)	(2.8)	(3.0)	(4.2)	(4.4)	(2.8)	(2.5)	(1.9)	(1.0)
Exports	150.9	163.7	169.0	173.2	181.3	191.1	207.9	222.4	223.0	234.1
Imports	157.9	177.3	184.3	189.6	207.0	221.0	237.7	256.8	264.3	276.4
Foreign balance	−7.0	−13.6	−15.3	−16.5	−25.6	−29.8	−29.8	−34.4	−41.4	−42.3
	(0.7)	(−0.9)	(−0.2)	(−0.1)	(−1.1)	(−0.5)	(0.0)	(−0.5)	(−0.7)	(−0.1)
GDP (market prices)	769.4	790.0	810.6	834.3	860.4	895.4	921.7	941.4	953.2	962.0
	(1.0)	(2.7)	(2.6)	(2.9)	(3.1)	(4.1)	(2.9)	(2.1)	(1.3)	(0.9)

Note: Figures in parentheses are annual growth rates; for stockbuilding and the foreign balance they are contributions to GDP growth.
Source: ISTAT.

Table C. **Gross domestic product, by kind of activity**

Trillions of lire and percentage changes

	1983	1984	1985	1986	1987	1988	1989	1990	1991	1992
At current prices (trillions of lire)										
Agriculture	33.3	33.8	36.3	38.6	40.1	39.3	41.6	42.1	47.9	46.4
Industry[1]	185.1	210.8	234.0	256.8	277.3	308.8	337.2	360.8	374.9	387.7
Energy	29.0	33.8	37.5	43.6	48.1	52.5	57.5	67.0	75.1	82.6
Manufacturing	156.2	177.0	196.5	213.2	229.2	256.3	279.6	293.8	299.8	305.1
Construction	42.6	47.0	51.0	54.0	56.7	61.9	67.8	76.7	83.8	87.6
Services	364.2	423.4	479.0	542.3	594.9	662.3	725.2	815.1	895.5	975.6
Market services	282.7	330.9	375.9	428.8	469.0	520.3	571.2	634.5	697.4	766.6
Public administration	81.5	92.5	103.1	113.5	125.9	141.9	154.0	180.6	198.1	209.0
Subtotal	625.1	715.0	800.3	891.7	969.0	1 072.3	1 171.7	1 294.8	1 402.1	1 497.3
GDP (at market prices)	633.4	725.8	810.6	899.9	983.8	1 091.8	1 193.5	1 312.1	1 426.6	1 507.2
At 1985 prices (percentage changes)										
Agriculture	9.2	-4.8	0.8	1.9	3.7	-3.2	1.2	-2.9	7.5	1.3
Industry[1]	-0.2	3.7	2.7	3.0	3.7	6.5	3.5	2.3	-0.4	-0.5
Energy	-4.4	0.4	-0.5	5.8	2.0	1.8	2.4	4.1	0.8	0.8
Manufacturing	0.8	4.4	3.3	2.5	4.0	7.4	3.7	1.9	-0.6	-0.7
Construction	0.7	-3.3	0.1	0.6	1.4	2.6	3.5	2.5	1.3	-0.9
Services	1.2	3.4	3.1	3.1	2.9	3.5	2.9	2.5	1.6	2.3
Market services	1.2	4.0	3.5	3.6	3.4	4.1	3.4	2.9	1.8	2.7
Public administration	1.5	1.4	1.7	1.6	1.0	1.4	0.9	1.0	0.9	0.7
GDP (at market prices)	1.0	2.7	2.6	2.9	3.1	4.1	2.9	2.1	1.3	0.9

1. Including mining.
Source: ISTAT.

Table D. Household appropriation account
Trillions of lire

	1983	1984	1985	1986	1987	1988	1989	1990	1991	1992
Compensation of employees	300.2	335.0	374.1	404.1	438.8	482.6	528.3	593.2	647.7	681.0
Property and entrepreneurial income	241.8	274.4	296.5	337.3	363.8	401.6	449.4	496.0	555.3	602.4
Transfers received	138.0	154.0	176.6	194.3	213.7	237.5	264.5	297.5	326.7	359.3
Gross total income	680.0	763.4	847.1	935.7	1 016.3	1 121.7	1 242.3	1 386.7	1 529.6	1 642.7
Direct taxes	66.0	77.0	87.4	93.5	101.3	120.6	133.0	148.2	165.0	176.1
Social security contributions	117.8	130.7	148.3	170.6	180.8	199.2	224.8	253.7	286.1	303.6
Disposable income	496.2	555.7	611.4	671.6	734.2	801.8	884.5	984.9	1 078.6	1 162.9
Consumption	385.6	441.3	495.8	549.5	604.4	668.2	737.4	803.4	877.5	944.9
Savings ratio[1]	22.3	20.6	18.9	18.2	17.7	16.7	16.6	18.4	18.6	18.7
Real disposable income (percentage change)	4.4	0	1.0	3.4	3.8	3.3	3.7	4.8	2.5	2.2

1. As a percentage of disposable income.
Sources: OECD, based on ISCO and Bank of Italy estimates.

Table E. General Government account
Trillions of lire

	1983	1984	1985	1986	1987	1988	1989	1990	1991	1992
Current receipts	240.5	274.0	310.8	351.8	386.1	432.4	494.1	554.0	618.2	659.3
Direct taxes	78.4	91.4	105.5	115.7	130.6	145.7	170.7	189.1	207.0	220.9
Social security contributions	89.2	98.5	110.2	125.5	135.8	149.4	167.5	189.3	210.0	226.4
Indirect taxes	58.0	67.3	72.7	81.7	93.2	109.1	123.9	139.5	159.2	166.5
Other current receipts	14.9	16.7	22.4	28.9	26.5	28.3	32.1	36.1	42.0	45.4
Current expenditure	283.9	325.6	367.0	412.8	447.2	499.2	559.4	635.4	705.2	772.4
Expenditure on goods and services	103.2	118.0	133.3	146.0	163.9	184.3	198.5	228.4	249.8	263.1
Subsidies	18.1	22.2	22.8	27.7	26.1	26.6	29.8	29.6	32.5	30.9
Interest paid	48.0	58.1	65.1	76.4	78.2	88.9	106.6	126.1	145.4	171.8
Social benefits	109.7	121.6	139.1	154.8	170.5	189.1	210.0	238.6	261.4	288.5
Other current transfers	4.9	5.7	6.8	8.0	8.5	10.4	14.5	12.8	16.2	18.2
Saving	-43.4	-51.6	-56.2	-61.0	-61.1	-66.8	-65.3	-81.5	-87.1	-113.2
Fixed investment	23.5	26.2	30.4	31.9	34.5	36.8	39.8	43.1	46.2	44.5
Capital transfers, net	-2.3	-7.9	-17.4	-14.2	-15.2	-16.5	-16.9	-23.5	-18.1	8.2
Consumption of fixed capital	1.4	1.7	2.0	2.3	2.7	3.2	3.8	4.5	5.3	6.2
Net lending	-67.7	-84.0	-102.0	-104.7	-108.1	-116.8	-118.2	-143.6	-146.1	-143.3
(as a percentage of GDP)	-10.7	-11.6	-12.6	-11.6	-11.0	-10.7	-9.9	-10.9	-10.2	-9.5

Source: Relazione generale sulla situazione economica del paese (1990).

Table F. **Prices and wages**

	1983	1984	1985	1986	1987	1988	1989	1990	1991	1992
Indices, 1985 = 100										
Consumer prices										
Total	82.7	91.6	100.0	105.8	110.9	116.5	123.8	131.8	140.0	147.2
Food products	84.2	91.9	100.0	105.3	109.2	112.9	120.0	127.2	135.3	142.1
Non-food products	82.1	91.5	100.0	106.0	111.5	117.7	125.1	133.4	141.8	149.4
Services (excluding rent)	80.5	89.9	100.0	108.9	114.9	122.4	132.1	141.9	152.3	163.8
Per capita compensation										
Total economy										
Nominal	81.3	90.8	100.0	107.5	116.4	126.6	137.7	153.0	166.3	175.7
Real	98.3	99.2	100.0	101.6	105.0	108.7	111.3	116.1	118.8	119.4
Industry										
Nominal	78.9	89.7	100.0	107.5	115.6	124.9	137.6	150.5	164.4	174.7
Real	95.5	98.0	100.0	101.6	104.3	107.2	111.2	114.2	117.5	118.7
Percentage changes										
Consumer prices										
Total	14.6	10.8	9.2	5.8	4.7	5.1	6.3	6.5	6.2	5.2
Food products	11.7	9.2	8.8	5.3	3.6	3.5	6.3	6.0	6.4	5.0
Non-food products	15.9	11.4	9.3	6.0	5.1	5.6	6.3	6.6	6.3	5.4
Services (excluding rent)	18.1	11.7	11.2	8.9	5.5	6.6	7.9	7.4	7.3	7.5
Per capita compensation										
Total economy										
Nominal	16.0	11.8	10.1	7.5	8.2	8.8	8.8	11.0	8.7	5.7
Real	1.2	0.9	0.8	1.6	3.3	3.5	2.4	4.3	2.3	0.5
Industry										
Nominal	16.0	13.7	11.4	7.5	7.5	8.0	10.2	9.3	9.3	6.2
Real	1.2	2.6	2.0	1.6	2.6	2.8	3.7	2.7	2.9	1.0

Sources: ISTAT; OECD, National Accounts.

Table G. **Employment indicators**

Labour units, thousands

	1983	1984	1985	1986	1987	1988	1989	1990	1991	1992
Total employment	22 325	22 412	22 613	22 787	22 877	23 074	23 088	23 272	23 450	23 245
Dependent employment	15 211	15 187	15 404	15 473	15 528	15 700	15 795	15 971	16 042	15 961
Agriculture	827	792	784	767	749	734	747	741	712	723
Total industry	5 970	5 698	5 614	5 544	5 500	5 554	5 557	5 591	5 487	5 327
of which: Manufacturing	4 565	4 343	4 281	4 228	4 212	4 264	4 281	4 284	4 169	4 005
Construction	1 217	1 166	1 141	1 120	1 089	1 092	1 080	1 110	1 123	1 133
Market services	4 532	4 736	4 967	5 091	5 150	5 214	5 269	5 387	5 543	5 560
General government	3 882	3 960	4 038	4 071	4 129	4 198	4 222	4 252	4 301	4 352
Self-employment	7 114	7 225	7 209	7 314	7 349	7 373	7 293	7 300	7 408	7 283
of which: Agriculture	1 918	1 894	1 796	1 796	1 759	1 662	1 530	1 494	1 525	1 419
Total industry	1 378	1 306	1 300	1 327	1 308	1 315	1 322	1 325	1 347	1 343
Market services	3 818	4 025	4 113	4 191	4 283	4 396	4 441	4 482	4 537	4 521

Source: ISTAT.

161

Table H. Money and credit

a) The monetary base

Changes in billions of lire

	1983	1984	1985	1986	1987	1988	1989	1990	1991	1992
Origin of liquid assets										
Net impact of the foreign sector	8 840	5 141	-13 677	3 543	6 756	10 947	14 971	15 458	-8 674	-32 591
Net impact of the public sector	4 514	10 027	27 519	10 994	9 172	2 748	6 344	1 008	17 715	40 086
Banks	-3	-218	5 881	-4 333	-730	-30	1 203	1 260	2 664	121
Other sectors	-747	-1 104	-646	-1 004	-1 252	-709	-2 042	-4 027	-583	857
Total net impact	12 604	13 846	19 076	9 199	13 947	12 956	20 475	13 700	11 121	8 473
Use of liquid assets										
Liquidity in the hands of the public	4 079	3 851	4 004	3 140	4 382	4 449	10 477	1 805	6 906	9 263
Compulsory bank reserves	9 092	8 855	12 213	9 022	8 740	9 444	9 567	13 026	3 424	1 012
Bank liquidity	360	1 142	2 858	-2 962	167	-280	431	-1 131	791	-1 802
Compulsory bank deposits	-927	-2	..	..	657	-657	..	..	..	..
Total	12 604	13 846	19 076	9 199	13 947	12 956	20 475	13 700	11 121	8 473

Source: Banca d'Italia, *Annual Report.*

Table H. Money and credit

b) Selected indicators

Changes in billions of lire

	1983	1984	1985	1986	1987	1988	1989	1990	1991	1992
Money[1]										
Currency in circulation[2]	3 944	3 662	3 807	3 107	4 126	4 733	10 269	1 805	6 906	9 263
Sight deposits	23 238	26 701	24 569	29 981	21 987	24 154	37 038	30 379	45 879	699
Saving deposits	21 697	24 671	27 581	20 518	26 530	30 027	34 531	37 175	37 434	49 617
Money supply M2	48 879	55 035	55 957	53 605	52 643	58 913	81 828	63 596	76 113	41 795
Central bank										
Credit to Treasury	1 264	13 728	27 461	10 943	6 575	2 278	6 673	1 383	9 458	2 696
Credit to banking sector	2 768	-1 530	5 673	-3 360	327	478	917	1 621	1 054	557
Banking sector										
Credit	24 713	38 290	28 410	22 821	22 878	54 281	75 766	73 639	73 818	46 688
Government securities shares and bonds	27 834	13 027	15 388	14 573	7 567	-10 629	-3 348	-7 460	16 362	19 180
Special credit institutions										
Credit	14 401	15 768	10 336	16 801	22 217	27 525	36 608	39 601	38 230	35 003
Total domestic credit	121 273	145 151	153 435	152 676	151 991	197 171	230 600	235 448	260 862	263 387
Private sector	36 076	53 442	46 168	45 967	46 119	77 418	131 225	135 623	117 671	117 882

1. Data refers to households and firms only.
2. Excluding banking sector.
Source: Banca d'Italia, *Annual Report.*

163

Table I. **Foreign trade by main commodity groups**

Billions of Lire

	1983	1984	1985	1986	1987	1988	1989	1990	1991	1992
Imports, total	121 978	148 162	172 809	148 994	162 353	180 014	209 910	217 703	225 746	232 111
Agricultural products	9 943	11 848	14 258	12 866	13 271	14 045	15 164	14 314	15 955	14 828
Energy	38 028	41 825	46 224	23 853	22 698	19 095	24 324	27 460	26 894	24 807
Iron, steel and non-ferrous metals	10 160	13 703	14 976	13 805	13 959	17 561	22 709	20 569	19 466	19 625
Minerals and non-metallic mineral products	1 766	2 227	2 482	2 507	2 829	3 427	3 913	4 205	4 391	4 498
Chemical products	12 450	15 603	18 576	18 477	19 655	23 108	26 191	27 004	27 487	29 085
Manufactured goods	17 240	22 071	27 070	29 237	34 918	41 635	46 150	49 375	51 623	52 704
Transport equipment	8 332	11 043	13 306	13 744	16 481	18 539	22 839	25 823	28 803	32 551
Food, beverages and tobacco	10 511	11 705	15 052	13 804	14 169	15 228	16 971	16 766	18 002	18 799
Textile products	5 621	7 544	9 231	9 174	10 788	12 081	13 670	13 855	14 550	15 747
Other imports	7 927	10 593	11 634	11 527	13 585	15 295	17 979	18 332	18 575	19 467
Exports, total	110 530	129 027	149 724	145 331	150 879	166 380	192 813	203 515	209 728	219 436
Agricultural products	3 510	3 836	4 688	4 198	4 187	4 532	5 026	5 359	6 005	5 791
Energy	6 147	6 177	7 161	4 132	3 759	3 240	3 725	4 609	4 718	4 708
Iron, steel and non-ferrous metals	5 763	6 965	7 890	6 863	6 517	7 900	9 786	9 348	8 960	9 086
Minerals and non-metallic mineral products	4 791	5 431	5 771	5 702	6 065	7 123	8 183	8 491	8 665	9 144
Chemical products	8 770	11 056	12 785	11 698	12 397	14 283	15 646	15 445	15 620	17 346
Manufactured goods	34 685	39 394	46 044	46 896	49 569	55 112	65 490	69 026	71 990	75 181
Transport equipment	10 393	11 171	12 410	13 200	14 153	15 967	19 008	21 611	22 141	21 903
Food, beverages and tobacco	4 371	5 586	7 054	6 099	6 267	6 981	7 780	8 133	9 056	10 414
Textile products	20 035	24 571	28 893	29 764	30 272	30 872	34 565	37 202	36 952	38 582
Other exports	12 065	14 840	17 028	16 779	17 693	20 370	23 604	24 291	25 621	27 281

Source: Istituto nazionale per il Commercio Estero, *Rapporto sul Commercio Estero*, 1992.

Table J. Geographical breakdown of foreign trade
Million US dollars

	1983	1984	1985	1986	1987	1988	1989	1990	1991	1992
Imports, total	80 325	84 338	90 506	99 976	124 682	138 984	162 269	193 541	189 576	188 339
OECD countries	49 083	53 178	58 126	73 839	94 060	107 250	123 398	147 857	145 211	145 536
EEC	35 784	38 243	42 790	55 584	70 696	80 155	92 294	111 351	109 459	110 750
of which: Germany	12 872	13 527	15 179	20 625	26 489	30 480	34 626	41 255	39 657	40 609
Belgium-Luxembourg	2 718	3 103	3 360	4 641	6 197	6 795	8 033	9 854	9 245	9 120
France	10 114	10 472	11 281	14 559	18 203	20 631	23 842	27 541	26 857	27 224
Netherlands	3 912	4 117	4 606	5 883	6 971	7 957	8 915	11 098	10 897	11 127
United Kingdom	3 127	3 668	4 473	5 102	6 569	7 076	7 864	10 111	10 778	10 779
USA	4 771	5 146	5 392	5 685	6 650	7 791	8 846	9 868	10 596	9 855
Canada	523	583	526	574	827	975	1 217	1 546	1 449	1 470
Japan	1 112	1 348	1 481	2 093	2 668	3 512	3 742	4 504	4 640	4 402
Non OECD countries	31 167	30 985	32 072	25 747	30 446	31 487	38 621	45 350	43 989	42 281
COMECON	5 178	5 989	4 810	3 979	4 918	5 394	6 446	7 056	7 347	7 719
OPEC	14 818	13 270	14 387	9 473	10 245	8 099	10 335	13 648	13 544	11 593
Others	11 171	11 726	12 874	12 295	15 283	17 993	21 840	24 646	23 099	22 969
Exports, total	72 777	73 431	78 400	97 479	116 085	128 458	149 053	180 927	176 126	178 055
OECD countries	49 905	52 136	57 654	76 206	93 243	103 485	118 990	145 329	139 896	137 700
EEC	35 401	34 966	37 941	52 395	65 350	73 771	84 615	105 755	104 070	102 829
of which: Germany	12 155	11 960	12 759	17 867	21 803	23 468	25 647	34 604	36 966	36 240
Belgium-Luxembourg	2 092	2 125	2 327	3 248	3 918	4 337	4 875	6 165	5 987	5 906
France	10 701	10 289	11 000	15 229	18 958	21 308	24 285	29 622	26 749	26 014
Netherlands	2 178	2 111	2 425	3 190	3 580	3 956	4 618	5 640	5 555	5 582
United Kingdom	4 621	4 960	5 459	6 908	8 636	10 323	11 756	12 803	11 731	11 678
USA	5 618	8 003	9 617	10 472	11 159	11 427	12 858	13 812	12 142	12 410
Canada	637	808	978	1 199	1 350	1 437	1 650	1 605	1 441	1 295
Japan	791	843	925	1 319	1 855	2 425	3 407	4 239	3 861	3 418
Non OECD countries	22 087	20 565	19 969	20 730	22 322	24 431	29 481	34 890	35 465	39 739
COMECON	2 655	2 367	2 531	2 701	3 372	3 395	4 323	5 185	5 073	6 569
OPEC	9 885	8 602	7 262	6 210	5 867	6 020	7 130	7 397	8 372	9 178
Others	9 547	9 596	10 175	11 819	13 084	15 015	18 027	22 307	22 020	23 992

Source: OECD, Foreign Trade Statistics, Series B.

Table K. Balance of payments

Million US dollars

	1983	1984	1985	1986	1987	1988	1989	1990	1991	1992
Current account										
Merchandise exports	72 056	73 790	75 686	96 395	115 879	127 387	140 082	169 217	168 384	177 594
Merchandise imports	74 500	79 627	81 933	92 181	116 181	128 540	142 237	168 857	169 128	175 116
Trade balance	-2 444	-5 837	-6 247	4 214	-302	-1 153	-2 155	360	-744	2 478
Services, net	2 657	1 893	1 581	-222	-278	-3 151	-6 391	-12 443	-14 667	-23 151
Travel	7 211	6 496	6 474	6 944	7 634	6 414	5 214	5 910	6 772	4 924
Investment income	-3 896	-3 902	-3 979	-6 210	-6 610	-7 127	-8 286	-13 351	-16 114	-20 810
Other services	-658	-701	-914	-956	-1 302	-2 438	-3 319	-5 002	-5 325	-7 265
Transfers, net	1 513	1 643	1 085	-1 551	-1 013	-1 552	-2 492	-2 756	-6 028	-5 896
Private	1 467	1 471	1 347	1 507	1 208	1 276	1 309	835	-1 367	-1 840
Official	46	172	-262	-3 058	-2 221	-2 828	-3 801	-3 591	-4 661	-4 056
Current balance	1 726	-2 301	-3 581	2 441	-1 593	-5 856	-11 039	-14 838	-21 439	-26 569
Capital account										
Long-term capital, net	999	1 651	2 645	-2 588	2 469	7 899	22 569	37 497	2 892	-13 325
Private, direct	-933	-683	-749	-2 673	1 805	1 328	46	-1 268	-4 845	-2 795
Private, portfolio	232	99	375	-1 043	-7 416	331	3 463	-281	-6 094	-9 223
Public[1]	1 836	2 542	2 300	1 833	4 463	2 204	950	4 749	-1 404	106
Short-term capital, net	2 682	1 475	-1 994	5 094	6 169	8 735	2 347	6 015	20 301	22 888
Private non monetary	-606	-1 450	781	766	1 872	881	-1 684	1 509	-790	394
Private monetary institutions	3 288	2 925	-2 775	4 328	4 297	7 854	4 031	4 506	21 091	22 494
Miscellaneous official accounts	98	-208	181	210	-115	-847	93	-1 207	-6 111	10 597
Allocation of SDRs	0	0	0	0	0	0	0	0	0	0
Errors and omissions	378	2 132	-4 219	-2 607	-1 821	-2 400	-2 660	-16 026	-8 663	-9 412
Change in reserves	4 586	2 647	-4 124	-437	4 573	8 270	9 983	11 201	-13 599	-8 389

1. Excludes special transactions.
Source: OECD.

166

Table L. **Public sector**

Per cent of GDP

A. Budget indicators: general government accounts				
	1970	1980	1985	1990
Current receipts	27.9	32.3	37.3	41.1
Non-interest expenditures	31.3	36.5	42.9	43.6
Primary budget balance	–3.5	–4.2	–5.6	–2.4
Net interest	–0.6	–4.3	–7.0	–8.5
General government budget balance	–4.0	–8.6	–12.6	–10.9
of which:				
Central government	0.0	–7.2	–12.6	–9.9
Social security	0.0	–0.2	0.1	0.3
General government gross debt	41.7	59.0	84.3	100.5

B. Structure of expenditure and taxation				
1. General government expenditure				
	1970	1980	1985	1990
Expenditure: total	33.0	41.9	50.9	53.2
Current consumption	13.3	15.0	16.7	17.6
Tranfers to households	12.8	14.9	18.0	19.2
Subsidies	2.0	2.9	2.8	2.3
Fixed investment	3.2	3.2	3.7	3.3

2. Tax structure	Italy		EEC	
	1980	1989	1980	1989
Tax receipts	30.2	37.8	36.4	39.9
Income tax	9.4	14.0	12.5	13.8
of which:				
Personal income tax	7.0	10.1	10.6	10.4
Corporate profits tax	2.4	3.8	2.5	3.0
Social security contributions	11.5	12.5	10.5	11.3
Tax on goods and services	8.0	10.2	11.2	12.6

Source: OECD, *National accounts; Revenue statistics of OECD countries.*

Table M. **Financial markets**

	1970	1980	1985	1988
Financial institutions plus insurance sector [1]				
Sectoral employment over total employment (per cent)	1.0	1.6	1.7	1.7
Domestic net assets/GDP (per cent)	120.9	131.1	131.7	117.9
Structure of financial assets				
Share of financial institutions' financial assets in domestic assets (per cent) [2]	39.9	36.2	34.8	34.1
Share of Treasury securities in NFC total assets (per cent) [3]	0.5	1.9	3.6	5.7
Structure of NFC portfolios:				
Deposits (as per cent of total NFC financial assets)	57.4	29.2	19.5	18.2
Corporate bonds (as per cent of total NFC liabilities)	0.2	0.1	0.3	0.4
Mutual fund shares (as per cent of total NFC financial assets) [4]	–	–	–	–
Structure of non-financial corporate liabilities [5]				
NFC debt/equity ratio (per cent)				
Short-term: [2] Securities and mortgages	–	0.7	0.1	0.1
Other	48.1	51.5	47.3	47.3
Long-term: [2] Bonds	12.4	7.3	5.3	5.4
Other	37.1	39.8	32.6	33.0
Debt (per cent of GDP)				
Public sector				
Domestic	40.2	58.1	81.8	93.5
Foreign	1.1	0.9	2.2	2.7

1. Banca d'Italia, commercial banks, specialised credit institutions, finance companies, mutual funds, insurance companies.
2. Non-consolidated.
3. Including unincorporated enterprises.
4. Mutual fund certificates can be bought only by individuals and life insurance companies.
5. Excluding shares.
Source: Data submitted by national authorities.

Table N. **Labour market indicators**

	A. Evolution			
	Cyclical peak 1979	Cyclical trough 1982	1980	1990
Standardised unemployment rate	7.6	8.4	7.5	10.3
Unemployment rate				
Total	7.6	8.4	7.5	11.0
Male	4.8	5.6	4.7	7.3
Female	13.1	13.9	13.0	17.1
Youth[1]	25.6	28.0	25.2	31.5
Regional unemployment rate				
North-Centre	7.7	9.1	7.6	7.7
South	10.9	13.0	11.5	19.7
Share of long-term unemployment[2]	n.a.	n.a.	n.a.	69.3
Hours worked, 1980 = 100[3]	98.3	99.2	100.0	103.3

	B. Structural or institutional characteristics			
	1970	1980	1985	1990
Participation rate[4]				
Global	59.5	60.8	59.8	61.1
Male	86.8	82.8	79.3	78.1
Female	33.5	39.6	41.0	44.5
Employment/population between 15 and 64 years	54.7	54.7	52.2	54.6
Part-time work[5]	n.a.	n.a.	5.3	n.a.
Non-wage labour costs[6]	21.4	21.8	22.0	22.8
Government unemployment insurance benefits[7]	4.6	7.9	10.1	4.7

	1970-80	1980-85	1985-90
Employment (yearly rates of change)			
Total (persons)	0.6	0.2	0.5
Total (labour units)	1.0	0.5	0.7
Agriculture	–2.3	–2.9	–3.8
Manufacturing	1.0	–3.2	0.0
Services	2.7	3.3	1.7
of which:			
Government	2.8	2.1	1.1

1. People between 16 and 24 years as a percentage of the labour force of the same age group.
2. People looking for a job since one year or more as a percentage of total unemployment.
3. Index of monthly hours effectively worked per worker in industry.
4. Labour force as a percentage of the corresponding population aged between 16 and 64 years.
5. As a percentage of dependent employment.
6. As a percentage of wages and salaries.
7. Unemployment benefits per unemployed worker as a per cent of compensation per employee.
Sources: ISTAT and OECD.

169

Table O. **Production structure and performance indicators**

	GDP share (% of total)				Employment share (% of total)			
	1970	1980	1985	1990	1970	1980	1985	1990
Production structure (constant prices)								
Tradeable goods and services								
Agriculture	7.3	5.5	5.2	4.4	22.0	16.3	13.9	11.7
Manufacturing	24.0	28.6	28.2	28.8	31.5	32.4	27.3	26.6
of which:								
Food, beverage and tobacco	2.8	3.2	3.0	3.1	2.4	2.4	2.1	2.0
Textiles, wearing apparel and leather industries	4.7	5.3	4.9	4.7	7.8	7.4	6.4	6.1
Non-metallic mineral products except products								
of petroleum and coal	1.8	2.1	1.8	2.0	2.3	2.1	1.7	2.0
Basic metal industries	1.9	1.2	1.2	1.0	1.3	1.2	1.0	0.9
Fabricated metal products, machinery								
and equipment	10.2	11.7	9.7	9.4	10.2	11.7	9.7	9.4
Non-tradeable goods and services								
Electricity, gas and water	7.5	6.3	5.4	5.3	1.0	1.0	1.0	1.0
Construction	12.6	8.4	7.3	6.9	11.8	9.6	8.9	8.6
Wholesale and retail trade, restaurants								
and hotels	21.5	22.1	22.2	21.6	19.9	22.6	25.8	26.1
Transport, storage, communications	5.2	5.9	6.3	6.7	6.0	6.8	7.3	7.9
Finance, insurance, real estate and business sector	22.3	23.3	25.5	26.1	7.8	11.3	15.8	18.1

Productivity growth
(Sector GDP/sector employment)
Average annual percentage growth

	1971-80	1981-85	1986-90
Industrial sector (constant prices)			
Manufacturing	4.7	4.4	3.8
of which:			
Food, beverage and tobacco	4.5	2.9	4.0
Textiles, wearing apparel and leather industries	4.9	2.9	2.9
Non-metallic mineral products except products			
of petroleum and coal	6.1	1.9	1.9
Basic metal industries	-0.8	5.8	2.6
Fabricated metal products, machinery			
and equipment	4.5	4.6	4.3

Source: OECD, National Accounts.

BASIC STATISTICS

BASIC STATISTICS:

INTERNATIONAL COMPARISONS

	Units	Reference period[1]	Australia	Austria	Belgium	Canada
Population						
Total	Thousands	1990	17 085	7 718	9 967	26 620
Inhabitants per sq. km	Number	1990	2	92	327	3
Net average annual increase over previous 10 years	%	1990	1.5	0.2	0.1	1
Employment						
Total civilian employment (TCE)[2]	Thousands	1990	7 850	3 412	3 726	12 572
Of which : Agriculture	% of TCE		5.6	7.9	2.7	4.2
Industry	% of TCE		25.4	36.8	28.3	24.6
Services	% of TCE		69	55.3	69	71.2
Gross domestic product (GDP)						
At current prices and current exchange rates	Bill US $	1990	294.1	157.4	192.4	570.1
Per capita	US $		17 215	20 391	19 303	21 418
At current prices using current PPP's[3]	Bill US $	1990	271.7	127.4	163	510.5
Per capita	US $		15 900	16 513	16 351	19 179
Average annual volume growth over previous 5 years	%	1990	3.1	3.1	3.2	3
Gross fixed capital formation (GFCF)	% of GDP	1990	22.9	24.3	20.3	21.4
Of which: Machinery and equipment	% of GDP		9.7	10.1	10.4	7.2
Residential construction	% of GDP	1990	4.8	4.6	4.3	6.8
Average annual volume growth over previous 5 years	%	1990	2.4	4.6	9.5	5.8
Gross saving ratio[4]	% of GDP	1990	19.7	26	21.8	17.4
General government						
Current expenditure on goods and services	% of GDP	1990	17.3	18	14.3	19.8
Current disbursements[5]	% of GDP	1990	34.9	44.9	53.1	44
Current receipts	% of GDP	1990	35.1	46.7	49.5	41.6
Net official development assistance	Mill US $	1990	0.34	0.25	0.45	0.44
Indicators of living standards						
Private consumption per capita using current PPP's[3]	US $	1990	9 441	9 154	10 119	11 323
Passenger cars per 1 000 inhabitants	Number	1989	570	416	416	613
Telephones per 1 000 inhabitants	Number	1989	550 (85)	540	500 (88)	780 (88)
Television sets per 1 000 inhabitants	Number	1988	217	484 (89)	255	586
Doctors per 1 000 inhabitants	Number	1990	2.3	2.1	3.4	2.2
Infant mortality per 1 000 live births	Number	1990	8.2	7.8	7.9	7.2 (89)
Wages and prices (average annual increase over previous 5 years)						
Wages (earnings or rates according to availability)	%	1990	5.6	5	3	4.3
Consumer prices	%	1990	7.9	2.2	2.1	4.5
Foreign trade						
Exports of goods, fob*	Mill US $	1990	39 813	40 985	118 291[7]	127 334
As % of GDP	%		13.5	26	61.5	22.3
Average annual increase over previous 5 years	%		11.9	19.1	17.1	7.8
Imports of goods, cif*	Mill US $	1990	38 907	48 914	120 330[7]	116 561
As % of GDP	%		13.2	31.1	62.5	20.4
Average annual increase over previous 5 years	%		11	18.6	16.5	8.8
Total official reserves[6]	Mill SDR's	1990	11 432	6 591	8 541[7]	12 544
As ratio of average monthly imports of goods	ratio		3.5	1.6	0.9	1.3

* At current prices and exchange rates.
1. Unless otherwise stated.
2. According to the definitions used in OECD Labour Force Statistics.
3. PPP's = Purchasing Power Parities.
4. Gross saving = Gross national disposable income minus Private and Government consumption.
5. Current disbursements = Current expenditure on goods and services plus current transfers and payments of property income.
6. Gold included in reserves is valued at 35 SDR's per ounce. End of year.
7. Including Luxembourg.
8. Included in Belgium.

EMPLOYMENT OPPORTUNITIES

Economics Department, OECD

The Economics Department of the OECD offers challenging and rewarding opportunities to economists interested in applied policy analysis in an international environment. The Department's concerns extend across the entire field of economic policy analysis, both macro-economic and micro-economic. Its main task is to provide, for discussion by committees of senior officials from Member countries, documents and papers dealing with current policy concerns. Within this programme of work, three major responsibilities are:

- to prepare regular surveys of the economies of individual Member countries;
- to issue full twice-yearly reviews of the economic situation and prospects of the OECD countries in the context of world economic trends;
- to analyse specific policy issues in a medium-term context for theOECD as a whole, and to a lesser extent for the non-OECD countries.

The documents prepared for these purposes, together with much of the Department's other economic work, appear in published form in the *OECD Economic Outlook, OECD Economic Surveys, OECD Economic Studies* and the Department's *Working Papers* series.

The Department maintains a world econometric model, INTERLINK, which plays an important role in the preparation of the policy analyses and twice-yearly projections. The availability of extensive cross-country data bases and good computer resources facilitates comparative empirical analysis, much of which is incorporated into the model.

The Department is made up of about 75 professional economists from a variety of backgrounds and Member countries. Most projects are carried out by small teams and last from four to eighteen months. Within the Department, ideas and points of view are widely discussed; there is a lively professional interchange, and all professional staff have the opportunity to contribute actively to the programme of work.

Skills the Economics Department is looking for:

a) Solid competence in using the tools of both micro-economic and macro-economic theory to answer policy questions. Experience indicates that this normally requires the equivalent of a PH.D. in economics or substantial relevant professional experience to compensate for a lower degree.

b) Solid knowledge of economic statistics and quantitative methods; this includes how to identify data, estimate structural relationships, apply basic techniques of time series analysis, and test hypotheses. It is essential to be able to interpret results sensibly in an economic policy context.

c) A keen interest in and knowledge of policy issues, economic developments and their political/social contexts.

d) Interest and experience in analysing questions posed by policy-makers and presenting the results to them effectively and judiciously. Thus, work experience in government agencies or policy research institutions is an advantage.

e) The ability to write clearly, effectively, and to the point. The OECD is a bilingual organisation with French and English as the official languages. Candidates must have excellent knowledge of one of these languages, and some knowledge of the other. Knowledge of other languages might also be an advantage for certain posts.

f) For some posts, expertise in a particular area may be important, but a successful candidate is expected to be able to work on a broader range of topics relevant to the work of the Department. Thus, except in rare cases, the Department does not recruit narrow specialists.

g) The Department works on a tight time schedule and strict deadlines. Moreover, much of the work in the Department is carried out in small groups of economists. Thus, the ability to work with other economists from a variety of cultural and professional backgrounds, to supervise junior staff, and to produce work on time is important.

General Information

The salary for recruits depends on educational and professional background. Positions carry a basic salary from FF 262 512 or FF 323 916 for Administrators (economists) and from FF 375 708 for Principal Administrators (senior economists). This may be supplemented by expatriation and/or family allowances, depending on nationality, residence and family situation. Initial appointments are for a fixed term of two to three years.

Vacancies are open to candidates from OECD Member countries. The Organisation seeks to maintain an appropriate balance between female and male staff and among nationals from Member countries.

For further information on employment opportunities in the Economics Department, contact:

Administrative Unit
Economics Department
OECD
2, rue André-Pascal
75775 PARIS CEDEX 16
FRANCE

Applications citing "ECSUR", together with a detailed *curriculum vitae* in English or French, should be sent to the Head of Personnel at the above address.

MAIN SALES OUTLETS OF OECD PUBLICATIONS
PRINCIPAUX POINTS DE VENTE DES PUBLICATIONS DE L'OCDE

ARGENTINA – ARGENTINE
Carlos Hirsch S.R.L.
Galería Güemes, Florida 165, 4° Piso
1333 Buenos Aires   Tel. (1) 331.1787 y 331.2391
Telefax: (1) 331.1787

AUSTRALIA – AUSTRALIE
D.A. Information Services
648 Whitehorse Road, P.O.B 163
Mitcham, Victoria 3132   Tel. (03) 873.4411
Telefax: (03) 873.5679

AUSTRIA – AUTRICHE
Gerold & Co.
Graben 31
Wien I   Tel. (0222) 533.50.14

BELGIUM – BELGIQUE
Jean De Lannoy
Avenue du Roi 202
B-1060 Bruxelles   Tel. (02) 538.51.69/538.08.41
Telefax: (02) 538.08.41

CANADA
Renouf Publishing Company Ltd.
1294 Algoma Road
Ottawa, ON K1B 3W8   Tel. (613) 741.4333
Telefax: (613) 741.5439
Stores:
61 Sparks Street
Ottawa, ON K1P 5R1   Tel. (613) 238.8985
211 Yonge Street
Toronto, ON M5B 1M4   Tel. (416) 363.3171
Telefax: (416)363.59.63

Les Éditions La Liberté Inc.
3020 Chemin Sainte-Foy
Sainte-Foy, PQ G1X 3V6   Tel. (418) 658.3763
Telefax: (418) 658.3763

Federal Publications Inc.
165 University Avenue, Suite 701
Toronto, ON M5H 3B8   Tel. (416) 860.1611
Telefax: (416) 860.1608

Les Publications Fédérales
1185 Université
Montréal, QC H3B 3A7   Tel. (514) 954.1633
Telefax : (514) 954.1635

CHINA – CHINE
China National Publications Import
Export Corporation (CNPIEC)
16 Gongti E. Road, Chaoyang District
P.O. Box 88 or 50
Beijing 100704 PR   Tel. (01) 506.6688
Telefax: (01) 506.3101

DENMARK – DANEMARK
Munksgaard Book and Subscription Service
35, Nørre Søgade, P.O. Box 2148
DK-1016 København K   Tel. (33) 12.85.70
Telefax: (33) 12.93.87

FINLAND – FINLANDE
Akateeminen Kirjakauppa
Keskuskatu 1, P.O. Box 128
00100 Helsinki
Subscription Services/Agence d'abonnements :
P.O. Box 23
00371 Helsinki   Tel. (358 0) 12141
Telefax: (358 0) 121.4450

FRANCE
OECD/OCDE
Mail Orders/Commandes par correspondance:
2, rue André-Pascal
75775 Paris Cedex 16   Tel. (33-1) 45.24.82.00
Telefax: (33-1) 45.24.81.76 or (33-1) 45.24.85.00
Telex: 640048 OCDE

OECD Bookshop/Librairie de l'OCDE :
33, rue Octave-Feuillet
75016 Paris   Tel. (33-1) 45.24.81.67
(33-1) 45.24.81.81
Documentation Française
29, quai Voltaire
75007 Paris   Tel. 40.15.70.00
Gibert Jeune (Droit-Économie)
6, place Saint-Michel
75006 Paris   Tel. 43.25.91.19
Librairie du Commerce International
10, avenue d'Iéna
75016 Paris   Tel. 40.73.34.60
Librairie Dunod
Université Paris-Dauphine
Place du Maréchal de Lattre de Tassigny
75016 Paris   Tel. (1) 44.05.40.13
Librairie Lavoisier
11, rue Lavoisier
75008 Paris   Tel. 42.65.39.95
Librairie L.G.D.J. - Montchrestien
20, rue Soufflot
75005 Paris   Tel. 46.33.89.85
Librairie des Sciences Politiques
30, rue Saint-Guillaume
75007 Paris   Tel. 45.48.36.02
P.U.F.
49, boulevard Saint-Michel
75005 Paris   Tel. 43.25.83.40
Librairie de l'Université
12a, rue Nazareth
13100 Aix-en-Provence   Tel. (16) 42.26.18.08
Documentation Française
165, rue Garibaldi
69003 Lyon   Tel. (16) 78.63.32.23
Librairie Decitre
29, place Bellecour
69002 Lyon   Tel. (16) 72.40.54.54

GERMANY – ALLEMAGNE
OECD Publications and Information Centre
August-Bebel-Allee 6
D-53175 Bonn 2   Tel. (0228) 959.120
Telefax: (0228) 959.12.17

GREECE – GRÈCE
Librairie Kauffmann
Mavrokordatou 9
106 78 Athens   Tel. (01) 32.55.321
Telefax: (01) 36.33.967

HONG-KONG
Swindon Book Co. Ltd.
13–15 Lock Road
Kowloon, Hong Kong   Tel. 366.80.31
Telefax: 739.49.75

HUNGARY – HONGRIE
Euro Info Service
POB 1271
1464 Budapest   Tel. (1) 111.62.16
Telefax : (1) 111.60.61

ICELAND – ISLANDE
Mál Mog Menning
Laugavegi 18, Pósthólf 392
121 Reykjavik   Tel. 162.35.23

INDIA – INDE
Oxford Book and Stationery Co.
Scindia House
New Delhi 110001   Tel.(11) 331.5896/5308
Telefax: (11) 332.5993
17 Park Street
Calcutta 700016   Tel. 240832

INDONESIA – INDONÉSIE
Pdii-Lipi
P.O. Box 269/JKSMG/88
Jakarta 12790   Tel. 583467
Telex: 62 875

IRELAND – IRLANDE
TDC Publishers – Library Suppliers
12 North Frederick Street
Dublin 1   Tel. (01) 874.48.35
Telefax: (01) 874.84.16

ISRAEL
Electronic Publications only
Publications électroniques seulement
Sophist Systems Ltd.
71 Allenby Street
Tel-Aviv 65134   Tel. 3-29.00.21
Telefax: 3-29.92.39

ITALY – ITALIE
Libreria Commissionaria Sansoni
Via Duca di Calabria 1/1
50125 Firenze   Tel. (055) 64.54.15
Telefax: (055) 64.12.57
Via Bartolini 29
20155 Milano   Tel. (02) 36.50.83
Editrice e Libreria Herder
Piazza Montecitorio 120
00186 Roma   Tel. 679.46.28
Telefax: 678.47.51
Libreria Hoepli
Via Hoepli 5
20121 Milano   Tel. (02) 86.54.46
Telefax: (02) 805.28.86
Libreria Scientifica
Dott. Lucio de Biasio 'Aeiou'
Via Coronelli, 6
20146 Milano   Tel. (02) 48.95.45.52
Telefax: (02) 48.95.45.48

JAPAN – JAPON
OECD Publications and Information Centre
Landic Akasaka Building
2-3-4 Akasaka, Minato-ku
Tokyo 107   Tel. (81.3) 3586.2016
Telefax: (81.3) 3584.7929

KOREA – CORÉE
Kyobo Book Centre Co. Ltd.
P.O. Box 1658, Kwang Hwa Moon
Seoul   Tel. 730.78.91
Telefax: 735.00.30

MALAYSIA – MALAISIE
Co-operative Bookshop Ltd.
University of Malaya
P.O. Box 1127, Jalan Pantai Baru
59700 Kuala Lumpur
Malaysia   Tel. 756.5000/756.5425
Telefax: 757.3661

MEXICO – MEXIQUE
Revistas y Periodicos Internacionales S.A. de C.V.
Florencia 57 - 1004
Mexico, D.F. 06600   Tel. 207.81.00
Telefax : 208.39.79

NETHERLANDS – PAYS-BAS
SDU Uitgeverij Plantijnstraat
Externe Fondsen
Postbus 20014
2500 EA's-Gravenhage   Tel. (070) 37.89.880
Voor bestellingen: Telefax: (070) 34.75.778

NEW ZEALAND
NOUVELLE-ZÉLANDE
Legislation Services
P.O. Box 12418
Thorndon, Wellington   Tel. (04) 496.5652
                            Telefax: (04) 496.5698

NORWAY – NORVÈGE
Narvesen Info Center – NIC
Bertrand Narvesens vei 2
P.O. Box 6125 Etterstad
0602 Oslo 6   Tel. (022) 57.33.00
                           Telefax: (022) 68.19.01

PAKISTAN
Mirza Book Agency
65 Shahrah Quaid-E-Azam
Lahore 54000   Tel. (42) 353.601
                          Telefax: (42) 231.730

PHILIPPINE – PHILIPPINES
International Book Center
5th Floor, Filipinas Life Bldg.
Ayala Avenue
Metro Manila   Tel. 81.96.76
                          Telex 23312 RHP PH

PORTUGAL
Livraria Portugal
Rua do Carmo 70-74
Apart. 2681
1200 Lisboa   Tel.: (01) 347.49.82/5
                         Telefax: (01) 347.02.64

SINGAPORE – SINGAPOUR
Information Publications Pte. Ltd.
41, Kallang Pudding, No. 04-03
Singapore 1334   Tel. 741.5166
                          Telefax: 742.9356

SPAIN – ESPAGNE
Mundi-Prensa Libros S.A.
Castelló 37, Apartado 1223
Madrid 28001   Tel. (91) 431.33.99
                          Telefax: (91) 575.39.98

Libreria Internacional AEDOS
Consejo de Ciento 391
08009 – Barcelona   Tel. (93) 488.30.09
                          Telefax: (93) 487.76.59
Llibreria de la Generalitat
Palau Moja
Rambla dels Estudis, 118
08002 – Barcelona
             (Subscripcions) Tel. (93) 318.80.12
             (Publicacions) Tel. (93) 302.67.23
                           Telefax: (93) 412.18.54

SRI LANKA
Centre for Policy Research
c/o Colombo Agencies Ltd.
No. 300-304, Galle Road
Colombo 3   Tel. (1) 574240, 573551-2
                   Telefax: (1) 575394, 510711

SWEDEN – SUÈDE
Fritzes Information Center
Box 16356
Regeringsgatan 12
106 47 Stockholm   Tel. (08) 690.90.90
                          Telefax: (08) 20.50.21
Subscription Agency/Agence d'abonnements :
Wennergren-Williams Info AB
P.O. Box 1305
171 25 Solna   Tel. (08) 705.97.50
                          Téléfax : (08) 27.00.71

SWITZERLAND – SUISSE
Maditec S.A. (Books and Periodicals - Livres
et périodiques)
Chemin des Palettes 4
Case postale 266
1020 Renens   Tel. (021) 635.08.65
                          Telefax: (021) 635.07.80

Librairie Payot S.A.
4, place Pépinet
CP 3212
1002 Lausanne   Tel. (021) 341.33.48
                          Telefax: (021) 341.33.45

Librairie Unilivres
6, rue de Candolle
1205 Genève   Tel. (022) 320.26.23
                          Telefax: (022) 329.73.18

Subscription Agency/Agence d'abonnements :
Dynapresse Marketing S.A.
38 avenue Vibert
1227 Carouge   Tel.: (022) 308.07.89
                          Telefax : (022) 308.07.99

See also – Voir aussi :
OECD Publications and Information Centre
August-Bebel-Allee 6
D-53175 Bonn 2 (Germany)   Tel. (0228) 959.120
                          Telefax: (0228) 959.12.17

TAIWAN – FORMOSE
Good Faith Worldwide Int'l. Co. Ltd.
9th Floor, No. 118, Sec. 2
Chung Hsiao E. Road
Taipei   Tel. (02) 391.7396/391.7397
                          Telefax: (02) 394.9176

THAILAND – THAÏLANDE
Suksit Siam Co. Ltd.
113, 115 Fuang Nakhon Rd.
Opp. Wat Rajbopith
Bangkok 10200   Tel. (662) 225.9531/2
                          Telefax: (662) 222.5188

TURKEY – TURQUIE
Kültür Yayinlari Is-Türk Ltd. Sti.
Atatürk Bulvari No. 191/Kat 13
Kavaklidere/Ankara   Tel. 428.11.40 Ext. 2458
Dolmabahce Cad. No. 29
Besiktas/Istanbul   Tel. 260.71.88
                          Telex: 43482B

UNITED KINGDOM – ROYAUME-UNI
HMSO
Gen. enquiries   Tel. (071) 873 0011
Postal orders only:
P.O. Box 276, London SW8 5DT
Personal Callers HMSO Bookshop
49 High Holborn, London WC1V 6HB
                          Telefax: (071) 873 8200
Branches at: Belfast, Birmingham, Bristol, Edin-
burgh, Manchester

UNITED STATES – ÉTATS-UNIS
OECD Publications and Information Centre
2001 L Street N.W., Suite 700
Washington, D.C. 20036-4910 Tel. (202) 785.6323
                          Telefax: (202) 785.0350

VENEZUELA
Libreria del Este
Avda F. Miranda 52, Aptdo. 60337
Edificio Galipán
Caracas 106   Tel. 951.1705/951.2307/951.1297
                   Telegram: Libreste Caracas

Subscription to OECD periodicals may also be
placed through main subscription agencies.

Les abonnements aux publications périodiques de
l'OCDE peuvent être souscrits auprès des
principales agences d'abonnement.

Orders and inquiries from countries where Distribu-
tors have not yet been appointed should be sent to:
OECD Publications Service, 2 rue André-Pascal,
75775 Paris Cedex 16, France.

Les commandes provenant de pays où l'OCDE n'a
pas encore désigné de distributeur devraient être
adressées à : OCDE, Service des Publications,
2, rue André-Pascal, 75775 Paris Cedex 16, France.

                                        12-1993

PRINTED IN FRANCE

•

OECD PUBLICATIONS
2 rue André-Pascal
75775 PARIS CEDEX 16
No. 46953
(10 94 19 1) ISBN 92-64-14054-9
ISSN 0376-6438

•